TEACHING A
STONE TO TALK

ANNIE DILLARD

TEACHING A STONE TO TALK

EXPEDITIONS AND ENCOUNTERS

HARPER & ROW, PUBLISHERS, New York
Cambridge, Philadelphia, San Francisco, London
Mexico City, São Paulo, Sydney

Portions of this work have appeared in *Antaeus, Atlantic Monthly, Christian Science Monitor, Harper's, The Living Wilderness, Potomac,* and *Self.*

"Expedition to the Pole" was first published in *The Yale Literary Magazine,* Volume 150, Number 1, June 1982.

Title page and chapter decorations: "Sun," The Granger Collection, New York.

FIRST EDITION

Designer: Gloria Adelson

Library of Congress Cataloging in Publication Data

Dillard, Annie.
   Teaching a stone to talk: expeditions and encounters.

   1. Nature. 2. Life. I. Title.
QH81.D563   508   82–47520
ISBN 0–06–015030–0   AACR2

82 83 84 85 86 10 9 8 7 6 5 4 3 2 1

For Gary

AUTHOR'S NOTE

Some of these have not been published before; others, such as "Living like Weasels" and "The Deer at Providencia," were published obscurely. At any rate, this is not a collection of occasional pieces, such as a writer brings out to supplement his real work; instead this is my real work, such as it is.

Contents

Living Like Weasels

A WEASEL IS WILD. Who knows what he thinks? He sleeps in his underground den, his tail draped over his nose. Sometimes he lives in his den for two days without leaving. Outside, he stalks rabbits, mice, muskrats, and birds, killing more bodies than he can eat warm, and often dragging the carcasses home. Obedient to instinct, he bites his prey at the neck, either splitting the jugular vein at the throat or crunching the brain at the base of the skull, and he does not let go. One naturalist refused to kill a weasel who was socketed into his hand deeply as a rattlesnake. The man could in no way pry the tiny weasel off, and he had to walk half a mile to water, the weasel dangling from his palm, and soak him off like a stubborn label.

And once, says Ernest Thompson Seton—once, a man shot an eagle out of the sky. He examined the eagle and found the dry skull of a weasel fixed by the jaws to his throat. The supposition is that the eagle had pounced on the weasel and the weasel swiveled and bit as instinct taught him, tooth to neck, and nearly won. I would like to have seen that eagle from the air a few weeks or months before he was shot: was the whole weasel still attached to his feathered throat, a fur pendant? Or did the eagle eat what he could reach, gutting the living weasel with his talons before his breast, bending his beak, cleaning the beautiful airborne bones?

I have been reading about weasels because I saw one last week. I startled a weasel who startled me, and we exchanged a long glance.

Twenty minutes from my house, through the woods by the quarry and across the highway, is Hollins Pond, a remarkable piece of shallowness, where I like to go at sunset and sit on a tree trunk. Hollins Pond is also called Murray's Pond; it covers two acres of bottomland near Tinker Creek with six inches of water and six thousand lily pads. In winter, brown-and-white steers stand in the middle of it, merely dampening their hooves; from the distant shore they look like miracle itself, complete with miracle's nonchalance. Now, in summer, the steers are gone. The water lilies have blossomed and spread to a green horizontal plane that is terra firma to plodding blackbirds, and tremulous ceiling to black leeches, crayfish, and carp.

This is, mind you, suburbia. It is a five-minute walk in three directions to rows of houses, though none is visible here. There's a 55 mph highway at one end of the pond, and a nesting pair of wood ducks at the other. Under every bush is a muskrat hole or a beer can. The far end is an alternating series of fields and woods, fields and woods, threaded everywhere with motorcycle tracks—in whose bare clay wild turtles lay eggs.

So. I had crossed the highway, stepped over two low barbed-wire fences, and traced the motorcycle path in all gratitude through the wild rose and poison ivy of the pond's shoreline up into high grassy fields. Then I cut down through the woods to the mossy fallen tree where I sit. This tree is excellent. It makes a dry, upholstered bench at the upper, marshy end of the pond, a plush jetty raised from the thorny shore between a shallow blue body of water and a deep blue body of sky.

The sun had just set. I was relaxed on the tree trunk, ensconced in the lap of lichen, watching the lily pads at my feet tremble and part dreamily over the thrusting path of a carp. A yellow bird appeared to my right and flew behind me. It caught my eye; I swiveled around— and the next instant, inexplicably, I was looking down at a weasel, who was looking up at me.

Weasel! I'd never seen one wild before. He was ten inches long, thin as a curve, a muscled ribbon, brown as fruitwood, soft-furred, alert. His face was fierce, small and pointed as a lizard's; he would have made a good arrowhead. There was just a dot of chin, maybe two brown hairs' worth, and then the pure white fur began that spread down his underside. He had two black eyes I didn't see, any more than you see a window.

The weasel was stunned into stillness as he was emerging from beneath an enormous shaggy wild rose bush four feet away. I was stunned into stillness twisted backward on the tree trunk. Our eyes locked, and someone threw away the key.

Our look was as if two lovers, or deadly enemies, met unexpectedly on an overgrown path when each had been thinking of something else: a clearing blow to the gut. It was also a bright blow to the brain, or a sudden beating of brains, with all the charge and intimate grate of rubbed balloons. It emptied our lungs. It felled the forest, moved the fields, and drained the pond; the world dismantled and tumbled into that black hole of eyes. If you and I looked at each other that way, our skulls would split and drop to our shoulders. But we don't. We keep our skulls. So.

He disappeared. This was only last week, and already I don't remember what shattered the enchantment. I think I blinked, I think I retrieved my brain from the weasel's brain, and tried to memorize what I was seeing, and the weasel felt the yank of separation, the careening splashdown into real life and the urgent current of instinct. He vanished under the wild rose. I waited motionless, my mind suddenly full of data and my spirit with pleadings, but he didn't return.

Please do not tell me about "approach-avoidance conflicts." I tell you I've been in that weasel's brain for sixty seconds, and he was in mine. Brains are private places, muttering through unique and secret tapes—but the weasel and I both plugged into another tape simultaneously, for a sweet and shocking time. Can I help it if it was a blank?

What goes on in his brain the rest of the time? What

does a weasel think about? He won't say. His journal is tracks in clay, a spray of feathers, mouse blood and bone: uncollected, unconnected, loose-leaf, and blown.

I would like to learn, or remember, how to live. I come to Hollins Pond not so much to learn how to live as, frankly, to forget about it. That is, I don't think I can learn from a wild animal how to live in particular—shall I suck warm blood, hold my tail high, walk with my footprints precisely over the prints of my hands?—but I might learn something of mindlessness, something of the purity of living in the physical senses and the dignity of living without bias or motive. The weasel lives in necessity and we live in choice, hating necessity and dying at the last ignobly in its talons. I would like to live as I should, as the weasel lives as he should. And I suspect that for me the way is like the weasel's: open to time and death painlessly, noticing everything, remembering nothing, choosing the given with a fierce and pointed will.

I missed my chance. I should have gone for the throat. I should have lunged for that streak of white under the weasel's chin and held on, held on through mud and into the wild rose, held on for a dearer life. We could live under the wild rose wild as weasels, mute and uncomprehending. I could very calmly go wild. I could live two days in the den, curled, leaning on mouse fur, sniffing bird bones, blinking, licking, breathing musk, my hair tangled in the roots of grasses. Down is a good place to go, where the mind is single. Down is out, out of your ever-loving mind and back to your careless senses.

I remember muteness as a prolonged and giddy fast, where every moment is a feast of utterance received. Time and events are merely poured, unremarked, and ingested directly, like blood pulsed into my gut through a jugular vein. Could two live that way? Could two live under the wild rose, and explore by the pond, so that the smooth mind of each is as everywhere present to the other, and as received and as unchallenged, as falling snow?

We could, you know. We can live any way we want. People take vows of poverty, chastity, and obedience— even of silence—by choice. The thing is to stalk your calling in a certain skilled and supple way, to locate the most tender and live spot and plug into that pulse. This is yielding, not fighting. A weasel doesn't "attack" anything; a weasel lives as he's meant to, yielding at every moment to the perfect freedom of single necessity.

I think it would be well, and proper, and obedient, and pure, to grasp your one necessity and not let it go, to dangle from it limp wherever it takes you. Then even death, where you're going no matter how you live, cannot you part. Seize it and let it seize you up aloft even, till your eyes burn out and drop; let your musky flesh fall off in shreds, and let your very bones unhinge and scatter, loosened over fields, over fields and woods, lightly, thoughtless, from any height at all, from as high as eagles.

An Expedition to the Pole

I

THERE IS A SINGING GROUP in this Catholic church today, a singing group which calls itself "Wildflowers." The lead is a tall, square-jawed teen-aged boy, buoyant and glad to be here. He carries a guitar; he plucks out a little bluesy riff and hits some chords. With him are the rest of the Wildflowers. There is an old woman, wonderfully determined; she has long orange hair and is dressed country-and-western style. A long embroidered strap around her neck slings a big western guitar low over her pelvis. Beside her stands a frail, withdrawn fourteen-year-old boy, and a large Chinese man in his twenties who seems to want to enjoy himself but is not quite sure how to. He looks around wildly as he sings, and shuffles his feet. There is also a very tall teen-aged girl, presumably the lead singer's girl friend; she is delicate of feature, half serene and half petrified, a wispy soprano. They straggle out in front of the altar and teach us a brand-new hymn.

It all seems a pity at first, for I have overcome a fiercely anti-Catholic upbringing in order to attend Mass simply and solely to escape Protestant guitars. Why am I here? Who gave these nice Catholics guitars? Why are they not mumbling in Latin and performing superstitious rituals? What is the Pope thinking of?

But nobody said things were going to be easy. A taste for the sublime is a greed like any other, after all; why begrudge the churches their secularism now, when from the general table is rising a general song? Besides, in a way I do not pretend to understand, these people—all the people in all the ludicrous churches—have access to the land.

The Land

The Pole of Relative Inaccessibility is "that imaginary point on the Arctic Ocean farthest from land in any direction." It is a navigator's paper point contrived to console Arctic explorers who, after Peary and Henson reached the North Pole in 1909, had nowhere special to go. There is a Pole of Relative Inaccessibility on the Antarctic continent, also; it is that point of land farthest from salt water in any direction.

The Absolute is the Pole of Relative Inaccessibility located in metaphysics. After all, one of the few things we know about the Absolute is that it is relatively inaccessible. It is that point of spirit farthest from every accessible point of spirit in all directions. Like the others, it is a Pole of the Most Trouble. It is also—I take this as given—the pole of great price.

The People

It is the second Sunday in Advent. For a year I have been attending Mass at this Catholic church. Every Sunday for a year I have run away from home and joined the circus as a dancing bear. We dancing bears have dressed ourselves in buttoned clothes; we mince around the rings on two feet. Today we were restless; we kept dropping onto our forepaws.

No one, least of all the organist, could find the opening hymn. Then no one knew it. Then no one could sing anyway.

There was no sermon, only announcements.

The priest proudly introduced the rascally acolyte who was going to light the two Advent candles. As we all could plainly see, the rascally acolyte had already lighted them.

During the long intercessory prayer, the priest always reads "intentions" from the parishioners. These are slips of paper, dropped into a box before the service begins, on which people have written their private concerns, by one, and we respond on cue. "For a baby safely delivered on November twentieth," the priest intoned, "we pray to the Lord." We all responded, "Lord, hear our prayer." Suddenly the priest broke in and confided to our bowed heads, "That's the baby we've been praying for the past two months! The woman just kept getting more and more pregnant!" How often, how shockingly often, have I exhausted myself in church from the effort to keep from laughing out loud? I often laugh all the way home. Then the priest read the next intention: "For my son, that he may forgive his father. We pray to the Lord." "Lord, hear our prayer," we responded, chastened.

A high school stage play is more polished than this service we have been rehearsing since the year one. In two thousand years, we have not worked out the kinks. We positively glorify them. Week after week we witness the same miracle: that God is so mighty he can stifle his own laughter. Week after week, we witness the same miracle: that God, for reasons unfathomable, refrains from blowing our dancing bear act to smithereens. Week after week Christ washes the disciples' dirty feet, handles their very toes, and repeats, It is all right—believe it or not—to be people.

Who can believe it?

During communion, the priest handed me a wafer which proved to be stuck to five other wafers. I waited while he tore the clump into rags of wafer, resisting the impulse to help. Directly to my left, and all through communion, a woman was banging out the theme from *The Sound of Music* on a piano.

The Land

Nineteenth-century explorers set the pattern for polar expeditions. Elaborately provisioned ships set out for high latitudes. Soon they encounter the pack ice and equinoctial storms. Ice coats the deck, spars, and rigging; the masts and hull shudder; the sea freezes around the rudder, and then fastens on the ship. Early sailors try ramming, sawing, or blasting the ice ahead of the ship before they give up and settle in for the winter. In the nineteenth century, this being "beset" in the pack often killed polar crews; later explorers expected it and learned, finally, to put it to use. Sometimes officers and men move directly onto the pack ice for safety; they drive tent stakes into the ice and pile wooden boxes about for tables and chairs.

Sooner or later, the survivors of that winter or the next, or a select polar party, sets off over the pack ice on foot. Depending on circumstances, they are looking either for a Pole or, more likely, for help. They carry supplies, including boats, on sledges which they "man-haul" on ropes fastened to shoulder harnesses. South Polar expeditions usually begin from a base camp established on shore. In either case, the terrain is so rough, and the men so weakened by scurvy, that the group makes only a few miles a day. Sometimes they find an island on which to live or starve the next winter; sometimes they turn back to safety, stumble onto some outpost of civilization, or are rescued by another expedition; very often, when warm weather comes and the pack ice splits into floes, they drift and tent on a floe, or hop from floe to floe, until the final floe lands, splits, or melts.

In 1847, according to Arctic historian L. P. Kirwan, the American ship *Polaris* "was struck by an enormous floe. And just as stores, records, clothing, equipment, were being flung from the reeling ship, she was swept away through the Arctic twilight, with most, but not all, of her crew on board. Those left behind drifted for thirteen hundred miles on an ice-floe until they were rescued, starving and dazed, off the coast of Labrador."

Polar explorers were chosen, as astronauts are today, from the clamoring, competitive ranks of the sturdy, skilled, and sane. Many of the British leaders, in particular, were men of astonishing personal dignity. Reading their accounts of life *in extremis,* one is struck by their unending formality toward each other. When Scott's Captain Oates sacrificed himself on the Antarctic peninsula because his ruined feet were slowing the march, he stepped outside the tent one night to freeze himself in a blizzard, saying to the others, "I am just going outside and may be some time."

Even in the privacy of their journals and diaries, polar explorers maintain a fine reserve. In his journal, Ernest Shackleton described his feelings upon seeing, for the first time in human history, the Antarctic continent beyond the mountains ringing the Ross Ice Shelf: "We watched the new mountains rise from the great unknown that lay ahead of us," he wrote, "with feelings of keen curiosity, not unmingled with awe." One wonders, after reading a great many such firsthand accounts, if polar explorers were not somehow chosen for the empty and solemn splendor of their prose styles—or even if some eminent Victorians, examining their own prose styles, realized, perhaps dismayed, that from the look of it, they would have to go in for polar exploration. Salomon Andrée, the doomed Swedish balloonist, was dying of starvation on an Arctic island when he confided in his diary, with almost his dying breath, "Our provisions must soon and richly be supplemented, if we are to have any prospect of being able to hold out for a time."

The People

The new Episcopalian and Catholic liturgies include a segment called "passing the peace." Many things can go wrong here. I know of one congregation in New York which fired its priest because he insisted on their passing the peace—which involves nothing more than shaking hands with your neighbors in the pew. The men and women of this small congregation had limits to their endurance; passing the peace was beyond their limits. They could not endure shaking hands with people to whom they bore lifelong grudges. They fired the priest and found a new one sympathetic to their needs.

The rubric for passing the peace requires that one shake hands with whoever is handy and say, "Peace be with you." The other responds, "Peace be with *you.*" Every rare once in a while, someone responds simply "Peace." Today I was sitting beside two teen-aged lugs with small mustaches. When it came time to pass the peace I shook hands with one of the lugs and said, "Peace be with you," and he said, *"Yeah."*

The Technology: The Franklin Expedition

The Franklin expedition was the turning point in Arctic exploration. The expedition itself accomplished nothing, and all its members died. But the expedition's failure to return, and the mystery of its whereabouts, attracted so much publicity in Europe and the United States that thirty ships set out looking for traces of the ships and men; these search parties explored and mapped the Arctic for the first time, found the northwest passage which Franklin had sought, and developed a technology adapted to Arctic conditions, a technology capable of bringing explorers back alive. The technology of the Franklin expedition, by contrast, was adapted only to conditions in the Royal Navy officers' clubs in England. The Franklin expedition stood on its dignity.

In 1845, Sir John Franklin and 138 officers and men embarked from England to find the northwest passage across the high Canadian Arctic to the Pacific Ocean. They sailed in two three-masted barques. Each sailing vessel carried an auxiliary steam engine and a twelve-day supply of coal for the entire projected two or three years' voyage. Instead of additional coal, according to L. P. Kirwan, each ship made room for a 1,200-volume library, "a hand-organ, playing fifty tunes," china place settings for officers and men, cut-glass wine goblets, and sterling silver flatware. The officers' sterling silver knives, forks, and spoons were particularly interesting. The silver was of ornate Victorian design, very heavy at the handles and richly patterned. Engraved on the handles were the individual officers' initials and family crests. The expedition carried no special clothing for the Arctic, only the uniforms of Her Majesty's Navy.

The ships set out in high dudgeon, amid enormous glory and fanfare. Franklin uttered his utterance: "The highest object of my desire is faithfully to perform my duty." Two months later a British whaling captain met the two barques in Lancaster Sound; he reported back to England on the high spirits of officers and men. He was the last European to see any of them alive.

Years later, civilization learned that many groups of Inuit—Eskimos—had hazarded across tableaux involving various still-living or dead members of the Franklin expedition. Some had glimpsed, for instance, men pushing and pulling a wooden boat across the ice. Some had found, at a place called Starvation Cove, this boat, or a similar one, and the remains of the thirty-five men who had been dragging it. At Terror Bay the Inuit found a tent on the ice, and in it, thirty bodies. At Simpson Strait some Inuit had seen a very odd sight: the pack ice pierced by the three protruding wooden masts of a barque.

For twenty years, search parties recovered skeletons from all over the frozen sea. Franklin himself—it was learned after twelve years—had died aboard ship. Franklin dead, the ships frozen into the pack winter after winter, their supplies exhausted, the remaining officers and men had decided to walk to help. They outfitted themselves from ships' stores for the journey; their bodies were found with those supplies they had chosen to carry. Accompanying one clump of frozen bodies, for instance, which incidentally showed evidence of cannibalism, were place settings of sterling silver flatware engraved with officers' initials and family crests. A search party found, on the ice far from the ships, a letter clip, and a piece of that very backgammon board which Lady Jane Franklin had given her husband as a parting gift.

Another search party found two skeletons in a boat on a sledge. They had hauled the boat sixty-five miles. With the two skeletons were some chocolate, some guns, some tea, and a great deal of table silver. Many miles south of these two was another skeleton, alone. This was a frozen officer. In his pocket he had, according to Kirwan, "a parody of a sea-shanty." The skeleton was in uniform: trousers and jacket "of fine blue cloth . . . edged with silk braid, with sleeves slashed and bearing five covered buttons each. Over this uniform the dead man had worn a blue greatcoat, with a black silk neckerchief." That was the Franklin expedition.

Sir Robert Falcon Scott, who died on the Antarctic peninsula, was never able to bring himself to use dogs, let alone feed them to each other or eat them. Instead he struggled with English ponies, for whom he carried hay. Scott felt that eating dogs was inhumane; he also felt, as he himself wrote, that when men reach a Pole unaided, their journey has "a fine conception" and "the conquest is more nobly and splendidly won." It is this loftiness of sentiment, this purity, this dignity and self-control, which makes Scott's farewell letters—found under his body—such moving documents.

Less moving are documents from successful polar expeditions. Their leaders relied on native technology, which, as every book ever written about the Inuit puts it, was "adapted to harsh conditions."

Roald Amundsen, who returned in triumph from the South Pole, traveled Inuit style; he made good speed using sleds and feeding dogs to dogs on a schedule. Robert E. Peary and Matthew Henson reached the North Pole in the company of four Inuit. Throughout the Peary expedition, the Inuit drove the dog teams, built igloos, and supplied seal and walrus clothing.

There is no such thing as a solitary polar explorer, fine as the conception is.

The People

I have been attending Catholic Mass for only a year. Before that, the handiest church was Congregational. Week after week I climbed the long steps to that little church, entered, and took a seat with some few of my neighbors. Week after week I was moved by the pitiableness of the bare linoleum-floored sacristy which no flowers could cheer or soften, by the terrible singing I so loved, by the fatigued Bible readings, the lagging emptiness and dilution of the liturgy, the horrifying vacuity of the sermon, and by the fog of dreary senselessness pervading the whole, which existed alongside, and probably caused, the wonder of the fact that we came; we returned; we showed up; week after week, we went through with it.

Once while we were reciting the Gloria, a farmer's wife—whom I knew slightly—and I exchanged a sudden, triumphant glance.

Recently I returned to that Congregational church for an ecumenical service. A Catholic priest and the minister served grape juice communion.

Both the priest and the minister were professionals, were old hands. They bungled with dignity and aplomb. Both were at ease and awed; both were half confident and controlled and half bewildered and whispering. I could hear them: "Where is it?" "Haven't you got it?" "I thought *you* had it!"

The priest, new to me, was in his sixties. He was tall; he wore his weariness loosely, standing upright and controlling his breath. When he knelt at the altar, and when he rose from kneeling, his knees cracked. It was a fine church music, this sound of his cracking knees.

The Land

Polar explorers—one gathers from their accounts—sought at the Poles something of the sublime. Simplicity and purity attracted them; they set out to perform clear tasks in uncontaminated lands. The land's austerity held them. They praised the land's spare beauty as if it were a moral or a spiritual quality: "icy halls of cold sublimity," "lofty peaks perfectly covered with eternal snow." Fridtjof Nansen referred to "the great adventure of the ice, deep and pure as infinity . . . the eternal round of the universe and its eternal death." Everywhere polar prose evokes these absolutes, these ideas of "eternity" and "perfection," as if they were some perfectly visible part of the landscape.

They went, I say, partly in search of the sublime, and they found it the only way it can be found, here or there—around the edges, tucked into the corners of the days. For they were people—all of them, even the British—and despite the purity of their conceptions, they man-hauled their humanity to the Poles.

They man-hauled their frail flesh to the Poles, and encountered conditions so difficult that, for instance, it commonly took members of Scott's South Polar party several hours each morning to put on their boots. Day and night they did miserable, niggling, and often fatal battle with frostbitten toes, diarrhea, bleeding gums, hunger, weakness, mental confusion, and despair.

They man-hauled their sweet human absurdity to the Poles. When Robert E. Peary and Matthew Henson reached the North Pole in 1909, Peary planted there in the frozen ocean, according to L. P. Kirwan, the flag of the Dekes: "the colours of the Delta Kappa Epsilon Fraternity at Bowdoin College, of which Peary was an alumnus."

Polar explorers must adapt to conditions. They must adapt, on the one hand, to severe physical limitations; they must adapt, on the other hand—like the rest of us—to ordinary emotional limitations. The hard part is in finding a workable compromise. If you are Peary and have planned your every move down to the last jot and tittle, you can perhaps get away with carrying a Deke flag to the North Pole, if it will make you feel good. After eighteen years' preparation, why not feel a little good? If you are an officer with the Franklin expedition and do not know what you are doing or where you are, but think you cannot eat food except from sterling silver tableware, you cannot get away with it. Wherever we go, there seems to be only one business at hand—that of finding workable compromises between the sublimity of our ideas and the absurdity of the fact of us.

They made allowances for their emotional needs. Overwintering expedition ships commonly carried, in *addition* to sufficient fuel, equipment for the publication of weekly newspapers. The brave polar men sat cooling their heels *in medias* nowhere, reading in cold type their own and their bunkmates' gossip, in such weeklies as Parry's *Winter Chronicle and North Georgia Gazette,* Nansen's *Framsjaa,* or Scott's *South Polar Times* and *The Blizzard.* Polar explorers also amused themselves with theatrical productions. If one had been frozen into the pack ice off Ross Island near Antarctica, aboard Scott's ship *Discovery,* one midwinter night in 1902, one could have seen the only performance of *Ticket of Leave, a screaming comedy in one act.* Similarly, if, in the dead of winter, 1819, one had been a member of young Edward Parry's expedition frozen into the pack ice in the high Arctic, one could have caught the first of a series of fortnightly plays, an uproarious success called *Miss in her Teens.* According to Kirwan, " 'This,' Parry dryly remarked, 'afforded to the men such a fund of amusement as fully to justify the expectations we had formed of the utility of theatrical entertainments.' " And you yourself, Royal Navy Commander Edward Parry, were you not yourself the least bit amused? Or at twenty-nine years old did you still try to stand on your dignity?

The Land

God does not demand that we give up our personal dignity, that we throw in our lot with random people, that we lose ourselves and turn from all that is not him. God needs nothing, asks nothing, and demands nothing, like the stars. It is a life with God which demands these things.

Experience has taught the race that if knowledge of God is the end, then these habits of life are not the means but the condition in which the means operates. You do not have to do these things; not at all. God does not, I regret to report, give a hoot. You do not have to do these things—unless you want to know God. They work on you, not on him.

You do not have to sit outside in the dark. If, however, you want to look at the stars, you will find that darkness is necessary. But the stars neither require nor demand it.

The Technology

It is a matter for computation: how far can one walk carrying how much silver? The computer balks at the problem; there are too many unknowns. The computer puts its own questions: Who is this "one"? What degree of stamina may we calculate for? Under what conditions does this one propose to walk, at what latitudes? With how many companions, how much aid?

The People

The Mass has been building to this point, to the solemn saying of those few hushed phrases known as the Sanctus. We have confessed, in a low, distinct murmur, our sins; we have become the people broken, and then the people made whole by our reluctant assent to the priest's proclamation of God's mercy. Now, as usual, we will, in the stillest voice, stunned, repeat the Sanctus, repeat why it is that we have come:

> Holy, holy, holy Lord,
> God of power and might,
> heaven and earth are full of your glory . . .

It is here, if ever, that one loses oneself at sea. Here, one's eyes roll up, and the sun rolls overhead, and the floe rolls underfoot, and the scene of unrelieved ice and sea rolls over the planet's pole and over the world's rim wide and unseen.

Now, just as we are dissolved in our privacy and about to utter the words of the Sanctus, the lead singer of Wildflowers bursts onstage from the wings. I raise my head. He is taking enormous, enthusiastic strides and pumping his guitar's neck up and down. Drooping after him come the orange-haired country-and-western-style woman; the soprano, who, to shorten herself, carries her neck forward like a horse; the withdrawn boy; and the Chinese man, who is holding a tambourine as if it had stuck by some defect to his fingers and he has resolved to forget about it. These array themselves in a clump downstage right. The priest is nowhere in sight.

Alas, alack, oh brother, we are going to have to *sing* the Sanctus. There is, of course, nothing new about singing the Sanctus. The lead singer smiles disarmingly. There is a new arrangement. He hits a chord with the flat of his hand. The Chinese man with sudden vigor bangs the tambourine and looks at his hands, startled. They run us through the Sanctus three or four times. The words are altered a bit to fit the strong upbeat rhythm:

> Heaven and earth
> (Heaven and earth earth earth earth earth)
> Are full (full full full)
> Of your glory . . .

Must I join this song? May I keep only my silver? My backgammon board, I agree, is a frivolity. I relinquish it. I will leave it right here on the ice. But my silver? My family crest? One knife, one fork, one spoon, to carry beneath the glance of heaven and back? I have lugged it around for years; I am, I say, superlatively strong. Don't laugh. I am superlatively strong! Don't laugh; you'll make *me* laugh. The answer is no. We are singing the Sanctus, it seems, and they are passing the plate. I would rather, I think, undergo the famous dark night of the soul than encounter in church the dread hootenanny—but these purely personal preferences are of no account, and maladaptive to boot. They are passing the plate and I toss in my schooling; I toss in my rank in the Royal Navy, my erroneous and incomplete charts, my pious refusal to eat sled dogs, my watch, my keys, and my shoes. I was looking for bigger game, not little moral lessons; but who can argue with conditions?

"Heaven and earth earth earth earth earth," we sing. The withdrawn boy turns his head toward a man in front of me, who must be his father. Unaccountably, the enormous teen-aged soprano catches my eye, exultant. A low shudder or shock crosses our floe. We have split from the pack; we have crossed the Arctic Circle, and the current has us.

The Land

We are clumped on an ice floe drifting over the black polar sea. Heaven and earth are full of our terrible singing. Overhead we see a blurred, colorless brightness; at our feet we see the dulled, swift ice and recrystallized snow. The sea is black and green; a hundred thousand floes and bergs float in the water and spin and scatter in the current around us everywhere as far as we can see. The wind is cool, moist, and scented with salt.

I am wearing, I discover, the uniform of a Keystone Kop. I examine my hat: a black cardboard constable's hat with a white felt star stapled to the band above the brim. My dark Keystone Kop jacket is nicely belted, and there is a tin badge on my chest. A holster around my hips carries a popgun with a cork on a string, and a red roll of caps. My feet are bare, but I feel no cold. I am skating around on the ice, and singing, and bumping into people who, because the ice is slippery, bump into other people. "Excuse me!" I keep saying, "I beg your pardon woops there!"

When a crack develops in our floe and opens at my feet, I jump across it—skillfully, I think—but my jump pushes my side of the floe away, and I wind up leaping full tilt into the water. The Chinese man extends a hand to pull me out, but alas, he slips and I drag him in. The Chinese man and I are treading water, singing, and collecting a bit of a crowd. It takes a troupe of circus clowns to get us both out. I check my uniform at once and learn that my rather flattering hat is intact, my trousers virtually unwrinkled, but my roll of caps is wet. The Chinese man is fine; we thank the clowns.

This troupe of circus clowns, I hear, is poorly paid. They are invested in bright, loose garments; they are a bunch of spontaneous, unskilled, oversized children; they joke and bump into people. At one end of the floe, ten of them—red, yellow, and blue—are trying to climb up on each other to make a human pyramid. It is a wonderfully funny sight, because they have put the four smallest clowns on the bottom, and the biggest, fattest clown is trying to climb to the top. The rest of the clowns are doing gymnastics; they tumble on the ice and flip cheerfully in midair. Their crucifixes fly from their ruffled necks as they flip, and hit them on their bald heads as they land. Our floe is smaller now, and we seem to have drifted into a faster bit of current. Repeatedly we ram little icebergs, which rock as we hit them. Some of them tilt clear over like punching bags; they bounce back with great splashes, and water streams down their blue sides as they rise. The country-and-western-style woman is fending off some of the larger bergs with a broom. The lugs with the mustaches have found, or brought, a Frisbee, and a game is developing down the middle of our floe. Near the Frisbee game, a bunch of people including myself and some clowns are running. We fling ourselves down on the ice, shoulders first, and skid long distances like pucks.

Now the music ceases and we take our seats in the pews. A baby is going to be baptized. Overhead the sky is brightening; I do not know if this means we have drifted farther north, or all night.

The People

The baby's name is Oswaldo; he is a very thin baby who looks to be about one. He never utters a peep; he looks grim, and stiff as a planked shad. His parents—his father carrying him—and his godparents, the priest, and two acolytes, are standing on the ice between the first row of pews and the linoleum-floored sacristy. I am resting my bare feet on the velvet prie-dieu—to keep those feet from playing on the ice during the ceremony.

Oswaldo is half Filipino. His mother is Filipino. She has a wide mouth with much lipstick, and wide eyes; she wears a tight black skirt and stiletto heels. The father looks like Ozzie Nelson. He has marcelled yellow hair, a bland, meek face, and a big, meek nose. He is wearing a brown leather flight jacket. The godparents are both Filipinos, one of whom, in a pastel denim jump suit, keeps mugging for the Instamatic camera which another family member is shooting from the aisle.

The baby has a little red scar below one eye. He is wearing a long white lace baptismal gown, blue tennis shoes with white rubber toes, and red socks.

The priest anoints the baby's head with oil. He addresses to the parents several articles of faith: "Do you believe in God, the Father Almighty, creator of Heaven and earth?" "Yes, we believe."

The priest repeats a gesture he says was Christ's, explaining that it symbolically opens the infant's five senses to the knowledge of God. Uttering a formal prayer, he lays his hand loosely over Oswaldo's face and touches in rapid succession his eyes, ears, nose, and mouth. The baby blinks. The priest, whose voice is sometimes lost in the ruff at his neck, or blown away by the wind, is formal and gentle in his bearing; he knows the kid is cute, but he is not going to sentimentalize the sacrament.

Since our floe spins, we in the pews see the broken floes and tilting bergs, the clogged, calm polar sea, and the variously lighted sky and water's rim, shift and revolve enormously behind the group standing around the baby. Once I think I see a yellowish polar bear spurting out of the water as smoothly as if climbing were falling. I see the bear splash and flow onto a distant floeberg which tilts out of sight.

Now the acolytes bring a pitcher, a basin, and a linen towel. The father tilts the rigid baby over the basin; the priest pours water from the pitcher over the baby's scalp; the mother sops the baby with the linen towel and wraps it over his head, so that he looks, proudly, as though he has just been made a swami.

To conclude, the priest brings out a candle, for the purpose, I think, of pledging everybody to Christian fellowship with Oswaldo. Actually, I do not know what it is for; I am not listening. I am watching the hands at the candlestick. Each of the principals wraps a hand around the brass candlestick: the two acolytes with their small, pale hands at its base, the two families—Oswaldo's and his godparents'—with their varicolored hands in a row, and the priest at the top, as though he has just won the bat toss at baseball. The baby rides high in his father's arms, pointing his heels in his tennis shoes, silent, wanting down. His father holds him firmly with one hand and holds the candlestick beside his wife's hand with the other. The priest and the seated members of Wildflowers start clapping then—a round of applause for everybody here on the ice!—so we clap.

II

Months have passed; years have passed. Whatever ground gained has slipped away. New obstacles arise, and faintness of heart, and dread.

The Land

Polar explorers commonly die of hypothermia, starvation, scurvy, or dysentery; less commonly they contract typhoid fever (as Stefansson did), vitamin A poisoning from polar bear liver, or carbon monoxide poisoning from incomplete combustion inside tents sealed by snow. Very commonly, as a prelude to these deaths, polar explorers lose the use of their feet; their frozen toes detach when they remove their socks.

Particularly vivid was the death of a certain Mr. Joseph Green, the astronomer on Sir James Cook's first voyage to high latitudes. He took sick aboard ship. One night "in a fit of the phrensy," as a contemporary newspaper reported, he rose from his bunk and "put his legs out of the portholes, which was the occasion of his death."

Vitus Bering, shipwrecked in 1740 on Bering Island, was found years later preserved in snow. An autopsy showed he had had many lice, he had scurvy, and had died of a "rectal fistula which forced gas gangrene into his tissues."

The bodies of various members of the Sir John Franklin expedition of 1845 were found over the course of twenty years, by thirty search expeditions, in assorted bizarre postures scattered over the ice of Victoria Strait, Beechey Island, and King William Island.

Sir Robert Falcon Scott reached the South Pole on January 17, 1912, only to discover a flag that Roald Amundsen had planted there a month earlier. Scott's body, and the bodies of two of his companions, turned up on the Ross Ice Shelf eleven miles south of one of their own supply depots. The bodies were in sleeping bags. His journals and farewell letters, found under his body, indicated that the other two had died first. Scott's torso was well out of his sleeping bag, and he had opened wide the collar of his parka, exposing his skin.

Never found were the bodies of Henry Hudson, his young son, and four men, whom mutineers in 1610 had lowered from their ship in a dinghy, in Hudson's Bay, without food or equipment. Never found were the bodies of Sir John Franklin himself, or of Amundsen and seventeen other men who set out for the Arctic in search of a disastrous Italian expedition, or the bodies of Scott's men Evans and Oates. Never found were most of the drowned crew of the United States ship *Polaris* or the body of her commander, who died sledging on the ice.

Of the United States Greely expedition to the North Pole, all men died but six. Greely himself, one of the six survivors, was found "on his hands and knees with long hair in pigtails." Of the United States De Long expedition to the North Pole in the *Jeannette,* all men died but two. Of the *Jeannette* herself and her equipment, nothing was found until three years after she sank, when,

on a beach on the other side of the polar basin, a Green-
lander discovered a pair of yellow oilskin breeches
stamped *Jeannette.*

The People

Why do we people in churches seem like cheerful,
brainless tourists on a packaged tour of the Absolute?

The tourists are having coffee and doughnuts on Deck
C. Presumably someone is minding the ship, correcting
the course, avoiding icebergs and shoals, fueling the en-
gines, watching the radar screen, noting weather reports
radioed in from shore. No one would dream of asking
the tourists to do these things. Alas, among the tourists
on Deck C, drinking coffee and eating doughnuts, we
find the captain, and all the ship's officers, and all the
ship's crew. The officers chat; they swear; they wink a
bit at slightly raw jokes, just like regular people. The
crew members have funny accents. The wind seems to
be picking up.

On the whole, I do not find Christians, outside of the
catacombs, sufficiently sensible of conditions. Does anyone have the foggiest idea what sort of power we so
blithely invoke? Or, as I suspect, does no one believe a
word of it? The churches are children playing on the
floor with their chemistry sets, mixing up a batch of TNT
to kill a Sunday morning. It is madness to wear ladies'
straw hats and velvet hats to church; we should all be
wearing crash helmets. Ushers should issue life preservers
and signal flares; they should lash us to our pews. For
the sleeping god may wake someday and take offense,

or the waking god may draw us out to where we can never return.

The eighteenth-century Hasidic Jews had more sense, and more belief. One Hasidic slaughterer, whose work required invoking the Lord, bade a tearful farewell to his wife and children every morning before he set out for the slaughterhouse. He felt, every morning, that he would never see any of them again. For every day, as he himself stood with his knife in his hand, the words of his prayer carried him into danger. After he called on God, God might notice and destroy him before he had time to utter the rest, "Have mercy."

Another Hasid, a rabbi, refused to promise a friend to visit him the next day: "How can you ask me to make such a promise? This evening I must pray and recite 'Hear, O Israel.' When I say these words, my soul goes out to the utmost rim of life. . . . Perhaps I shall not die this time either, but how can I now promise to do something at a time after the prayer?"

Assorted Wildlife

INSECTS

I like insects for their stupidity. A paper wasp—*Polistes*—is fumbling at the stained-glass window on my right. I saw the same sight in the same spot last Sunday: Pssst! Idiot! Sweetheart! Go around by the door! I hope we seem as endearingly stupid to God—bumbling down into lamps, running half-wit across the floor, banging for days at the hinge of an opened door. I hope so. It does not seem likely.

According to visitors, Antarctic penguins are . . . adorable. They are tame! They are funny!

Tourists in Antarctica are mostly women of a certain age. They step from the cruise ship's rubber Zodiacs wearing bright ship's-issue parkas; they stalk around on the gravel and squint into the ice glare; they exclaim over the penguins, whom they find tame, funny, and adorable; they take snapshots of each other with the penguins, and look around cheerfully for something else to look around at.

The penguins are adorable, and the wasp at the stained-glass window is adorable, because in each case their impersonations of human dignity so evidently fail. What are the chances that God finds our failed impersonation of human dignity adorable? Or is he fooled? What odds do you give me?

III

The Land

Several years ago I visited the high Arctic and saw it: the Arctic Ocean, the Beaufort Sea. The place was Barter Island, inside the Arctic Circle, in the Alaskan Arctic north of the North Slope. I stood on the island's ocean shore and saw what there was to see: a pile of colorless stripes. Through binoculars I could see a bigger pile of colorless stripes.

It seemed reasonable to call the colorless stripe overhead "sky," and reasonable to call the colorless stripe at my feet "ice," for I could see where it began. I could distinguish, that is, my shoes, and the black gravel shore, and the nearby frozen ice the wind had smashed ashore. It was this mess of ice—ice breccia, pressure ridges, and standing floes, ice sheets upright, tilted, frozen together and jammed—which extended out to the horizon. No matter how hard I blinked, I could not put a name to any of the other stripes. Which was the horizon? Was I seeing land, or water, or their reflections in low clouds? Was I seeing the famous "water sky," the "frost smoke," or the "ice blink"?

In his old age, James McNeill Whistler used to walk down to the Atlantic shore carrying a few thin planks and his paints. On the planks he painted, day after day, in broad, blurred washes representing sky, water, and shore, three blurry light-filled stripes. These are late Whistlers; I like them very much. In the high Arctic I thought of them, for I seemed to be standing in one of them. If I loosed my eyes from my shoes, the gravel at my feet, or the chaos of ice at the shore, I saw what newborn babies must see: nothing but senseless variations of light on the retinas. The world was a color-field painting wrapped round me at an unknown distance; I hesitated to take a step.

There was, in short, no recognizable three-dimensional space in the Arctic. There was also no time. The sun never set, but neither did it appear. The dim round-the-clock light changed haphazardly when the lid of cloud thickened or thinned. Circumstances made the eating of meals random or impossible. I slept when I was tired.

When I woke I walked out into the colorless stripes and the revolving winds, where atmosphere mingled with distance, and where land, ice, and light blurred into a dreamy, freezing vapor which, lacking anything else to do with the stuff, I breathed. Now and then a white bird materialized out of the vapor and screamed. It was, in short, what one might, searching for words, call a beautiful land; it was more beautiful still when the sky cleared and the ice shone in the dark water.

The Technology

It is for the Pole of Relative Inaccessibility I am searching, and have been searching, in the mountains and along the seacoasts for years. The aim of this expedition is, as Pope Gregory put it in his time, "To attain to somewhat of the unencompassed light, by stealth, and scantily." How often have I mounted this same expedition, has my absurd barque set out half-caulked for the Pole?

The Land

"These incidents are *true*," I read in an 1880 British history of Arctic exploration. "These incidents are *true*,— the storm, the drifting ice-raft, the falling berg, the sinking ship, the breaking up of the great frozen floe: these scenes are *real*,—the vast plains of ice, the ridged hummocks, the bird-thronged cliff, the far-stretching glacier."

Polar exploration is no longer the fashion it was during the time of the Franklin expedition, when beachgoers at Brighton thronged to panoramas of Arctic wastes painted in shopwindows, and when many thousands of Londoners jammed the Vauxhall pleasure gardens to see a diorama of polar seas. Our attention is elsewhere now, but the light-soaked land still exists; I have seen it.

The Technology

In the nineteenth century, a man deduced Antarctica. During that time, no one on earth knew for certain whether there was any austral land mass at all, although the American Charles Wilkes claimed to have seen it. Some geographers and explorers speculated that there was no land, only a frozen Antarctic Ocean; others posited two large islands in the vicinity of the Pole. That there is one continent was not in fact settled until 1935.

In 1893, one John Murray presented to the Royal Geographic Society a deduction of the Antarctic continent. His expedition's ship, the *Challenger*, had never come within sight of any such continent. His deduction proceeded entirely from dredgings and soundings. In his presentation he posited a large, single continent, a speculative map of which he furnished. He described accurately the unknown continent's topology: its central plateau with its permanent high-pressure system, its enormous glacier facing the Southern Ocean, its volcanic ranges at one coast, and at another coast, its lowland ranges and hills. He was correct.

Deduction, then, is possible—though no longer fashionable. There are many possible techniques for the exploration of high latitudes. There is, for example, such a thing as a drift expedition.

When that pair of yellow oilskin breeches belonging to the lost crew of the *Jeannette* turned up after three years in Greenland, having been lost north of central Russia, Norwegian explorer Fridtjof Nansen was interested. On the basis of these breeches' travels he plotted the probable direction of the current in the polar basin. Then he mounted a drift expedition: in 1893 he drove his ship, the *Fram,* deliberately into the pack ice and settled in to wait while the current moved north and, he hoped, across the Pole. For almost two years, he and a crew of twelve lived aboard ship as the frozen ocean carried them. Nansen wrote in his diary, "I long to return to life . . . the years are passing here . . . Oh! at times this inactivity crushes one's very soul; one's life seems as dark as the winter night outside; there is sunlight upon no other part of it except the past and the far, far distant future. I feel as if I *must* break through this deadness."

The current did not carry them over the Pole, so Nansen and one companion set out one spring with dog sledges and kayaks to reach the Pole on foot. Conditions were too rough on the ice, however, so after reaching a record northern latitude, the two turned south toward land, wintering together finally in a stone hut on Franz Josef Land and living on polar bear meat. The following spring they returned, after almost three years, to civilization.

Nansen's was the first of several drift expeditions. During World War I, members of a Canadian Arctic expedition camped on an ice floe seven miles by fifteen miles; they drifted for six months over four hundred miles in the Beaufort Sea. In 1937, an airplane deposited a Soviet drift expedition on an ice floe near the North Pole. These four Soviet scientists drifted for nine months while their floe, colliding with grounded ice, repeatedly split into ever-smaller pieces.

The Land

I have, I say, set out again.
The days tumble with meanings. The corners heap up with poetry; whole unfilled systems litter the ice.

The Technology

A certain Lieutenant Maxwell, a member of Vitus Bering's second polar expedition, wrote, "You never feel safe when you have to navigate in waters which are completely blank."

Cartographers call blank spaces on a map "sleeping beauties."

On our charts I see the symbol for shoals and beside it the letters "P.D." My neighbor in the pew, a lug with a mustache who has experience of navigational charts and who knows how to take a celestial fix, tells me that the initials stand for "Position Doubtful."

The Land

To learn the precise location of a Pole, choose a clear, dark night to begin. Locate by ordinary navigation the Pole's position within an area of several square yards. Then arrange on the ice in that area a series of loaded cameras. Aim the cameras at the sky's zenith; leave their shutters open. Develop the film. The film from that camera located precisely at the Pole will show the night's revolving stars as perfectly circular concentric rings.

The Technology

I have a taste for solitude, and silence, and for what Plotinus called "the flight of the alone to the Alone." I have a taste for solitude. Sir John Franklin had, apparently, a taste for backgammon. Is either of these appropriate to conditions?

You quit your house and country, quit your ship, and quit your companions in the tent, saying, "I am just going outside and may be some time." The light on the far side of the blizzard lures you. You walk, and one day you enter the spread heart of silence, where lands dissolve and seas become vapor and ices sublime under unknown stars. This is the end of the Via Negativa, the lightless edge where the slopes of knowledge dwindle, and love for its own sake, lacking an object, begins.

The Land

I have put on silence and waiting. I have quit my ship and set out on foot over the polar ice. I carry chronometer and sextant, tent, stove and fuel, meat and fat. For water I melt the pack ice in hatchet-hacked chips; frozen salt water is fresh. I sleep when I can walk no longer. I walk on a compass bearing toward geographical north.

I walk in emptiness; I hear my breath. I see my hand

and compass, see the ice so wide it arcs, see the planet's peak curving and its low atmosphere held fast on the dive. The years are passing here. I am walking, light as any handful of aurora; I am light as sails, a pile of colorless stripes; I cry "heaven and earth indistinguishable!" and the current underfoot carries me and I walk.

The blizzard is like a curtain; I enter it. The blown snow heaps in my eyes. There is nothing to see or to know. I wait in the tent, myself adrift and emptied, for weeks while the storm unwinds. One day it is over, and I pick up my tent and walk. The storm has scoured the air; the clouds have lifted; the sun rolls round the sky like a fish in a round bowl, like a pebble rolled in a tub, like a swimmer, or a melody flung and repeating, repeating enormously overhead on all sides.

My name is Silence. Silence is my bivouac, and my supper sipped from bowls. I robe myself mornings in loose strings of stones. My eyes are stones; a chip from the pack ice fills my mouth. My skull is a polar basin; my brain pan grows glaciers, and icebergs, and grease ice, and floes. The years are passing here.

Far ahead is open water. I do not know what season it is, know how long I have walked into the silence like a tunnel widening before me, into the horizon's spread arms which widen like water. I walk to the pack ice edge, to the rim which calves its floes into the black and green water; I stand at the edge and look ahead. A scurf of candle ice on the water's skin as far as I can see scratches the sea and crumbles whenever a lump of ice or snow bobs or floats through it. The floes are thick in the water, some of them large as lands. By my side is passing a flat pan of floe from which someone extends an oar. I hold the oar's blade and jump. I land on the long floe.

No one speaks. Here, at the bow of the floe, the bright clowns have staked themselves to the ice. With tent stakes and ropes they have lashed their wrists and ankles to the floe on which they lie stretched and silent, face up. Among the clowns, and similarly staked, are many boys and girls, some women, and a few men from various countries. One of the men is Nansen, the Norwegian explorer who drifted. One of the women repeatedly opens and closes her fists. One of the clowns has opened his neck ruffle, exposing his skin. For many hours I pass among these staked people, intending to return later and take my place.

Farther along I see that the tall priest is here, the priest who served grape juice communion at an ecumenical service many years ago, in another country. He is very old. Alone on a wind-streaked patch of snow he kneels, stands, and kneels, and stands, and kneels. Not far from him, at the floe's side, sitting on a packing crate, is the deducer John Murray. He lowers a plumb bob overboard and pays out the line. He is wearing the antique fur hat of a Doctor of Reason, such as Erasmus wears in his portrait; it is understood that were he ever to return and present his findings, he would be ridiculed, for his hat. Scott's Captain Oates is here; he has no feet. It is he who stepped outside his tent, to save his friends. Now on his dignity he stands and mans the sheet of a square linen sail; he has stepped the wooden mast on a hillock amidships.

From the floe's stern I think I hear music; I set out,

but it takes me several sleeps to get there. I am no longer using the tent. Each time I wake, I study the floe and the ocean horizon for signs—signs of the pack ice which we left behind, or of open water, or land, or any weather. Nothing changes; there is only the green sea and the floating ice, and the black sea in the distance speckled by bergs, and a steady wind astern which smells of unknown mineral salts, some ocean floor.

At last I reach the floe's broad stern, its enormous trailing coast, its throngs, its many cooking fires. There are children carrying babies, and men and women painting their skins and trying to catch their reflections in the water to leeward. Near the water's edge there is a wooden upright piano, and a bench with a telephone book on it. A woman is sitting on the telephone book and banging out the Sanctus on the keys. The wind is picking up. I am singing at the top of my lungs, for a lark.

Many clowns are here; one of them is passing out Girl Scout cookies, all of which are stuck together. Recently, I learn, Sir John Franklin and crew have boarded this floe, and so have the crews of the lost *Polaris* and the *Jeannette*. The men, whose antique uniforms are causing envious glances, are hungry. Some of them start roughhousing with the rascally acolyte. One crewman carries the boy on his back along the edge to the piano, where he abandons him for a clump of cookies and a seat on the bench beside the short pianist, whose bare feet, perhaps on account of the telephone book, cannot reach the pedals. She starts playing "The Sound of Music." "You know any Bach?" I say to the lady at the piano, whose legs seem to be highly involved with those of the hungry crewman; "You know any Mozart? Or maybe

'How Great Thou Art'?" A skeletal officer wearing a black silk neckerchief has located Admiral Peary, recognizable from afar by the curious flag he holds. Peary and the officer together are planning a talent show and skits. When they approach me, I volunteer to sing "Antonio Spangonio, That Bum Toreador" and/or to read a piece of short fiction; they say they will let me know later.

Christ, under the illusion that we are all penguins, is crouched down posing for snapshots. He crouches, in his robe, between the lead singer of Wildflowers, who is joyfully trying to determine the best angle at which to hold his guitar for the camera, and the farmer's wife, who keeps her eyes on her painted toenails until the Filipino godfather with the camera says "Cheese." The country-and-western woman, singing, succeeds in pressing a cookie upon the baby Oswaldo. The baby Oswaldo is standing in his lace gown and blue tennis shoes in the center of a circle of explorers, confounding them.

In my hand I discover a tambourine. Ahead as far as the brittle horizon, I see icebergs among the floes. I see tabular bergs and floebergs and dark cracks in the water between them. Low overhead on the underside of the thickening cloud cover are dark colorless stripes reflecting pools of open water in the distance. I am banging on the tambourine, and singing whatever the piano player plays; now it is "On Top of Old Smoky." I am banging the tambourine and belting the song so loudly that people are edging away. But how can any of us tone it down? For we are nearing the Pole.

In the Jungle

LIKE ANY OUT-OF-THE-WAY PLACE, the Napo River in the Ecuadorian jungle seems real enough when you are there, even central. Out of the way of *what?* I was sitting on a stump at the edge of a bankside palm-thatch village, in the middle of the night, on the headwaters of the Amazon. Out of the way of human life, tenderness, or the glance of heaven?

A nightjar in deep-leaved shadow called three long notes, and hushed. The men with me talked softly in clumps: three North Americans, four Ecuadorians who were showing us the jungle. We were holding cool drinks and idly watching a hand-sized tarantula seize moths that came to the lone bulb on the generator shed beside us.

It was February, the middle of summer. Green fireflies spattered lights across the air and illumined for seconds, now here, now there, the pale trunks of enormous, solitary trees. Beneath us the brown Napo River was rising, in all silence; it coiled up the sandy bank and tangled its foam in vines that trailed from the forest and roots that looped the shore.

Each breath of night smelled sweet, more moistened and sweet than any kitchen, or garden, or cradle. Each star in Orion seemed to tremble and stir with my breath. All at once, in the thatch house across the clearing behind us, one of the village's Jesuit priests began playing an alto recorder, playing a wordless song, lyric, in a minor key, that twined over the village clearing, that caught in the big trees' canopies, muted our talk on the bankside, and wandered over the river, dissolving downstream.

This will do, I thought. This will do, for a weekend, or a season, or a home.

Later that night I loosed my hair from its braids and combed it smooth—not for myself, but so the village girls could play with it in the morning.

We had disembarked at the village that afternoon, and I had slumped on some shaded steps, wishing I knew some Spanish or some Quechua so I could speak with the ring of little girls who were alternately staring at me and smiling at their toes. I spoke anyway, and fooled with my hair, which they were obviously dying to get their hands on, and laughed, and soon they were all braiding my hair, all five of them, all fifty fingers, all my hair, even my bangs. And then they took it apart and did it again, laughing, and teaching me Spanish nouns, and meeting my eyes and each other's with open delight, while their small brothers in blue jeans climbed down from the trees and began kicking a volleyball around with one of the North American men.

Now, as I combed my hair in the little tent, another of the men, a free-lance writer from Manhattan, was talking quietly. He was telling us the tale of his life, describing his work in Hollywood, his apartment in Manhattan, his house in Paris. . . . "It makes me wonder," he said, "what I'm doing in a tent under a tree in the village of Pompeya, on the Napo River, in the jungle of Ecuador." After a pause he added, "It makes me wonder why I'm going *back.*"

The point of going somewhere like the Napo River in Ecuador is not to see the most spectacular anything. It is simply to see what is there. We are here on the planet only once, and might as well get a feel for the place. We might as well get a feel for the fringes and hollows in which life is lived, for the Amazon basin, which covers half a continent, and for the life that—there, like anywhere else—is always and necessarily lived in detail: on the tributaries, in the riverside villages, sucking this particular white-fleshed guava in this particular pattern of shade.

What is there is interesting. The Napo River itself is wide (I mean wider than the Mississippi at Davenport) and brown, opaque, and smeared with floating foam and logs and branches from the jungle. White egrets hunch on shoreline deadfalls and parrots in flocks dart in and out of the light. Under the water in the river, unseen, are anacondas—which are reputed to take a few village toddlers every year—and water boas, stingrays, crocodiles, manatees, and sweet-meated fish.

Low water bares gray strips of sandbar on which the natives build tiny palm-thatch shelters, arched, the size of pup tents, for overnight fishing trips. You see these extraordinarily clean people (who bathe twice a day in the river, and whose straight black hair is always freshly washed) paddling down the river in dugout canoes, hugging the banks.

Some of the Indians of this region, earlier in the century, used to sleep naked in hammocks. The nights are cold. Gordon MacCreach, an American explorer in these Amazon tributaries, reported that he was startled to hear the Indians get up at three in the morning. He was even more startled, night after night, to hear them walk down to the river slowly, half asleep, and bathe in the water. Only later did he learn what they were doing: they were getting warm. The cold woke them; they warmed their skins in the river, which was always ninety degrees; then they returned to their hammocks and slept through the rest of the night.

The riverbanks are low, and from the river you see an unbroken wall of dark forest in every direction, from the Andes to the Atlantic. You get a taste for looking at trees: trees hung with the swinging nests of yellow troupials, trees from which ant nests the size of grain sacks hang like black goiters, trees from which seven-colored tanagers flutter, coral trees, teak, balsa and breadfruit, enormous emergent silk-cotton trees, and the pale-barked *samona* palms.

When you are inside the jungle, away from the river, the trees vault out of sight. It is hard to remember to look up the long trunks and see the fans, strips, fronds, and sprays of glossy leaves. Inside the jungle you are more likely to notice the snarl of climbers and creepers round the trees' boles, the flowering bromeliads and epiphytes in every bough's crook, and the fantastic silk-cotton tree trunks thirty or forty feet across, trunks buttressed in flanges of wood whose curves can make three high walls of a room—a shady, loamy-aired room where you would gladly live, or die. Butterflies, iridescent blue, striped, or clear-winged, thread the jungle paths at eye level. And at your feet is a swath of ants bearing triangular bits of green leaf. The ants with their leaves look like a wide fleet of sailing dinghies—but they don't quit. In either direction they wobble over the jungle floor as far as the eye can see. I followed them off the path as far as I dared, and never saw an end to ants or to those luffing chips of green they bore.

Unseen in the jungle, but present, are tapirs, jaguars, many species of snake and lizard, ocelots, armadillos, marmosets, howler monkeys, toucans and macaws and a hundred other birds, deer, bats, peccaries, capybaras, agoutis, and sloths. Also present in this jungle, but variously distant, are Texaco derricks and pipelines, and some of the wildest Indians in the world, blowgun-using Indians, who killed missionaries in 1956 and ate them.

Long lakes shine in the jungle. We traveled one of these in dugout canoes, canoes with two inches of freeboard, canoes paddled with machete-hewn oars chopped from buttresses of silk-cotton trees, or poled in the shallows with peeled cane or bamboo. Our part-Indian guide had cleared the path to the lake the day before; when we walked the path we saw where he had impaled the lopped head of a boa, open-mouthed, on a pointed stick by the canoes, for decoration.

This lake was wonderful. Herons, egrets, and ibises plodded the sawgrass shores, kingfishers and cuckoos clattered from sunlight to shade, great turkeylike birds fussed in dead branches, and hawks lolled overhead. There was all the time in the world. A turtle slid into the water. The boy in the bow of my canoe slapped stones at birds with a simple sling, a rubber thong and leather pad. He aimed brilliantly at moving targets, always, and always missed; the birds were out of range. He stuffed his sling back in his shirt. I looked around.

The lake and river waters are as opaque as rain-forest leaves; they are veils, blinds, painted screens. You see things only by their effects. I saw the shoreline water roil and the sawgrass heave above a thrashing *paichi*, an enormous black fish of these waters; one had been caught the previous week weighing 430 pounds. Piranha fish live in the lakes, and electric eels. I dangled my fingers in the water, figuring it would be worth it.

We would eat chicken that night in the village, and rice, yucca, onions, beets, and heaps of fruit. The sun would ring down, pulling darkness after it like a curtain. Twilight is short, and the unseen birds of twilight wistful, uncanny, catching the heart. The two nuns in their dazzling white habits—the beautiful-boned young nun and the warm-faced old—would glide to the open cane-and-thatch schoolroom in darkness, and start the children singing. The children would sing in piping Spanish, high-pitched and pure; they would sing "Nearer My God to Thee" in Quechua, very fast. (To reciprocate, we sang for them "Old MacDonald Had a Farm"; I thought they might recognize the animal sounds. Of course they thought we were out of our minds.) As the children became excited by their own singing, they left their log benches and swarmed around the nuns, hopping, smiling at us, everyone smiling, the nuns' faces bursting in their cowls, and the clear-voiced children still singing, and the palm-leafed roofing stirred.

The Napo River: it is not out of the way. It is *in* the way, catching sunlight the way a cup catches poured water; it is a bowl of sweet air, a basin of greenness, and of grace, and, it would seem, of peace.

The Deer at Providencia

THERE WERE FOUR OF US NORTH AMERICANS IN THE JUNGLE, in the Ecuadorian jungle on the banks of the Napo River in the Amazon watershed. The other three North Americans were metropolitan men. We stayed in tents in one riverside village, and visited others. At the village called Providencia we saw a sight which moved us, and which shocked the men.

The first thing we saw when we climbed the riverbank to the village of Providencia was the deer. It was roped to a tree on the grass clearing near the thatch shelter where we would eat lunch.

The deer was small, about the size of a whitetail fawn, but apparently full-grown. It had a rope around its neck and three feet caught in the rope. Someone said that the dogs had caught it that morning and the villagers were going to cook and eat it that night.

This clearing lay at the edge of the little thatched-hut village. We could see the villagers going about their business, scattering feed corn for hens about their houses, and wandering down paths to the river to bathe. The village headman was our host; he stood beside us as we watched the deer struggle. Several village boys were interested in the deer; they formed part of the circle we made around it in the clearing. So also did four businessmen from Quito who were attempting to guide us around the jungle. Few of the very different people standing in this circle had a common language. We watched the deer, and no one said much.

The deer lay on its side at the rope's very end, so the rope lacked slack to let it rest its head in the dust. It was "pretty," delicate of bone like all deer, and thin-skinned for the tropics. Its skin looked virtually hairless, in fact, and almost translucent, like a membrane. Its neck was no thicker than my wrist; it was rubbed open on the rope, and gashed. Trying to paw itself free of the rope, the deer had scratched its own neck with its hooves. The raw underside of its neck showed red stripes and some bruises bleeding inside the muscles. Now three of its feet were hooked in the rope under its jaw. It could not stand, of course, on one leg, so it could not move to slacken the rope and ease the pull on its throat and enable it to rest its head.

Repeatedly the deer paused, motionless, its eyes veiled, with only its rib cage in motion, and its breaths the only sound. Then, after I would think, "It has given up; now it will die," it would heave. The rope twanged; the tree leaves clattered; the deer's free foot beat the ground. We stepped back and held our breaths. It thrashed, kicking, but only one leg moved; the other three legs tightened inside the rope's loop. Its hip jerked; its spine shook. Its eyes rolled; its tongue, thick with spittle, pushed in and out. Then it would rest again. We watched this for fifteen minutes.

Once three young native boys charged in, released its trapped legs, and jumped back to the circle of people. But instantly the deer scratched up its neck with its hooves and snared its forelegs in the rope again. It was easy to imagine a third and then a fourth leg soon stuck, like Brer Rabbit and the Tar Baby.

We watched the deer from the circle, and then we drifted on to lunch. Our palm-roofed shelter stood on a grassy promontory from which we could see the deer tied to the tree, pigs and hens walking under village houses, and black-and-white cattle standing in the river. There was even a breeze.

Lunch, which was the second and better lunch we had that day, was hot and fried. There was a big fish called *doncella*, a kind of catfish, dipped whole in corn flour and beaten egg, then deep fried. With our fingers we pulled soft fragments of it from its sides to our plates, and ate; it was delicate fish-flesh, fresh and mild. Someone found the roe, and I ate of that too—it was fat and stronger, like egg yolk, naturally enough, and warm.

There was also a stew of meat in shreds with rice and

pale brown gravy. I had asked what kind of deer it was tied to the tree; Pepe had answered in Spanish, "*Gama.*" Now they told us this was *gama* too, stewed. I suspect the word means merely game or venison. At any rate, I heard that the village dogs had cornered another deer just yesterday, and it was this deer which we were now eating in full sight of the whole article. It was good. I was surprised at its tenderness. But it is a fact that high levels of lactic acid, which builds up in muscle tissues during exertion, tenderizes.

After the fish and meat we ate bananas fried in chunks and served on a tray; they were sweet and full of flavor. I felt terrific. My shirt was wet and cool from swimming; I had had a night's sleep, two decent walks, three meals, and a swim—everything tasted good. From time to time each one of us, separately, would look beyond our shaded roof to the sunny spot where the deer was still convulsing in the dust. Our meal completed, we walked around the deer and back to the boats.

That night I learned that while we were watching the deer, the others were watching me.

We four North Americans grew close in the jungle in a way that was not the usual artificial intimacy of travelers. We liked each other. We stayed up all that night talking, murmuring, as though we rocked on hammocks slung above time. The others were from big cities: New York, Washington, Boston. They all said that I had no expression on my face when I was watching the deer— or at any rate, not the expression they expected.

They had looked to see how I, the only woman, and the youngest, was taking the sight of the deer's struggles.

I looked detached, apparently, or hard, or calm, or focused, still. I don't know. I was thinking. I remember feeling very old and energetic. I could say like Thoreau that I have traveled widely in Roanoke, Virginia. I have thought a great deal about carnivorousness; I eat meat. These things are not issues; they are mysteries.

Gentlemen of the city, what surprises you? That there is suffering here, or that I know it?

We lay in the tent and talked. "If it had been my wife," one man said with special vigor, amazed, "she wouldn't have cared *what* was going on; she would have dropped *everything* right at that moment and gone in the village from here to there to there, she would not have *stopped* until that animal was out of its suffering one way or another. She couldn't *bear* to see a creature in agony like that."

I nodded.

Now I am home. When I wake I comb my hair before the mirror above my dresser. Every morning for the past two years I have seen in that mirror, beside my sleep-softened face, the blackened face of a burnt man. It is a wire-service photograph clipped from a newspaper and taped to my mirror. The caption reads: "Alan McDonald in Miami hospital bed." All you can see in the photograph is a smudged triangle of face from his eyelids to his lower lip; the rest is bandages. You cannot see the expression in his eyes; the bandages shade them.

The story, headed MAN BURNED FOR SECOND TIME, begins:

"Why does God hate me?" Alan McDonald asked from his hospital bed.

"When the gunpowder went off, I couldn't believe it," he said. "I just couldn't believe it. I said, 'No, God couldn't do this to me again.'"

He was in a burn ward in Miami, in serious condition. I do not even know if he lived. I wrote him a letter at the time, cringing.

He had been burned before, thirteen years previously, by flaming gasoline. For years he had been having his body restored and his face remade in dozens of operations. He had been a boy, and then a burnt boy. He had already been stunned by what could happen, by how life could veer.

Once I read that people who survive bad burns tend to go crazy; they have a very high suicide rate. Medicine cannot ease their pain; drugs just leak away, soaking the sheets, because there is no skin to hold them in. The people just lie there and weep. Later they kill themselves. They had not known, before they were burned, that the world included such suffering, that life could permit them personally such pain.

This time a bowl of gunpowder had exploded on McDonald.

"I didn't realize what had happened at first," he recounted. "And then I heard that sound from 13 years ago. I was burning. I rolled to put the fire out and I thought, 'Oh God, not again.'
"If my friend hadn't been there, I would have jumped into a canal with a rock around my neck."

His wife concludes the piece, "Man, it just isn't fair."

I read the whole clipping again every morning. This is the Big Time here, every minute of it. Will someone please explain to Alan McDonald in his dignity, to the deer at Providencia in his dignity, what is going on? And mail me the carbon.

When we walked by the deer at Providencia for the last time, I said to Pepe, with a pitying glance at the deer, *"Pobrecito"*—"poor little thing." But I was trying out Spanish. I knew at the time it was a ridiculous thing to say.

Teaching a Stone
to Talk

I

THE ISLAND WHERE I LIVE is peopled with cranks like my-self. In a cedar-shake shack on a cliff—but we all live like this—is a man in his thirties who lives alone with a stone he is trying to teach to talk.

Wisecracks on this topic abound, as you might expect, but they are made as it were perfunctorily, and mostly by the young. For in fact, almost everyone here respects what Larry is doing, as do I, which is why I am protecting his (or her) privacy, and confusing for you the details. It could be, for instance, a pinch of sand he is teaching to talk, or a prolonged northerly, or any one of a number

of waves. But it is, in fact, I assure you, a stone. It is—
for I have seen it—a palm-sized oval beach cobble whose
dark gray is cut by a band of white which runs around
and, presumably, through it; such stones we call "wishing
stones," for reasons obscure but not, I think, unimagina-
ble.

He keeps it on a shelf. Usually the stone lies protected
by a square of untanned leather, like a canary asleep
under its cloth. Larry removes the cover for the stone's
lessons, or more accurately, I should say, for the ritual
or rituals which they perform together several times a
day.

No one knows what goes on at these sessions, least
of all myself, for I know Larry but slightly, and that
owing only to a mix-up in our mail. I assume that like
any other meaningful effort, the ritual involves sacrifice,
the suppression of self-consciousness, and a certain precise tilt of the will, so that the will becomes transparent
and hollow, a channel for the work. I wish him well. It
is a noble work, and beats, from any angle, selling shoes.

Reports differ on precisely what he expects or wants
the stone to say. I do not think he expects the stone to
speak as we do, and describe for us its long life and
many, or few, sensations. I think instead that he is trying
to teach it to say a single word, such as "cup," or "uncle."
For this purpose he has not, as some have seriously sug-
gested, carved the stone a little mouth, or furnished it
in any way with a pocket of air which it might then
expel. Rather—and I think he is wise in this—he plans
to initiate his son, who is now an infant living with Larry's estranged wife, into the work, so that it may continue
and bear fruit after his death.

II

Nature's silence is its one remark, and every flake of world is a chip off that old mute and immutable block. The Chinese say that we live in the world of the ten thousand things. Each of the ten thousand things cries out to us precisely nothing.

God used to rage at the Israelites for frequenting sacred groves. I wish I could find one. Martin Buber says: "The crisis of all primitive mankind comes with the discovery of that which is fundamentally not-holy, the a-sacramental, which withstands the methods, and which has no 'hour,' a province which steadily enlarges itself." Now we are no longer primitive; now the whole world seems not-holy. We have drained the light from the boughs in the sacred grove and snuffed it in the high places and along the banks of sacred streams. We as a people have moved from pantheism to pan-atheism. Silence is not our heritage but our destiny; we live where we want to live.

The soul may ask God for anything, and never fail. You may ask God for his presence, or for wisdom, and receive each at his hands. Or you may ask God, in the words of the shopkeeper's little gag sign, that he not go away mad, but just go away. Once, in Israel, an extended family of nomads did just that. They heard God's speech and found it too loud. The wilderness generation was at Sinai; it witnessed there the thick darkness where God was: "and all the people saw the thunderings, and the lightnings, and the noise of the trumpet, and the mountain smoking." It scared them witless. Then they asked Moses to beg God, please, never speak to them directly again. "Let not God speak with us, lest we die." Moses took the message. And God, pitying their self-consciousness, agreed. He agreed not to speak to the people anymore. And he added to Moses, "Go say to them, Get into your tents again."

III

It is difficult to undo our own damage, and to recall to our presence that which we have asked to leave. It is hard to desecrate a grove and change your mind. The very holy mountains are keeping mum. We doused the burning bush and cannot rekindle it; we are lighting matches in vain under every green tree. Did the wind use to cry, and the hills shout forth praise? Now speech has perished from among the lifeless things of earth, and living things say very little to very few. Birds may crank out sweet gibberish and monkeys howl; horses neigh and pigs say, as you recall, oink oink. But so do cobbles rumble when a wave recedes, and thunders break the air in lightning storms. I call these noises silence. It could be that wherever there is motion there is noise, as when a whale breaches and smacks the water—and wherever there is stillness there is the still small voice, God's speaking from the whirlwind, nature's old song and dance, the show we drove from town. At any rate, now it is all we can do, and among our best efforts, to try to teach a given human language, English, to chimpanzees.

In the forties an American psychologist and his wife tried to teach a chimp actually to speak. At the end of three years the creature could pronounce, in a hoarse whisper, the words "mama," "papa," and "cup." After another three years of training she could whisper, with difficulty, still only "mama," "papa," and "cup." The more recent successes at teaching chimpanzees American Sign Language are well known. Just the other day a chimp told us, if we can believe that we truly share a vocabulary, that she had been sad in the morning. I'm sorry we asked. What have we been doing all these centuries but trying to call God back to the mountain, or, failing that, raise a peep out of anything that isn't us? What is the difference between a cathedral and a physics lab? Are not they both saying: Hello? We spy on whales and on interstellar radio objects; we starve ourselves and pray till we're blue.

IV

I have been reading comparative cosmology. At this time most cosmologists favor the picture of the evolving universe described by Lemaître and Gamow. But I prefer a suggestion made years ago by Valéry—Paul Valéry. He set forth the notion that the universe might be "head-shaped."

The mountains are great stone bells; they clang together like nuns. Who shushed the stars? There are a thousand million galaxies easily seen in the Palomar reflector; collisions between and among them do, of course, occur. But these collisions are very long and silent slides. Billions of stars sift among each other untouched, too distant even to be moved, heedless as always, hushed. The sea pronounces something, over and over, in a hoarse whisper; I cannot quite make it out. But God knows I have tried.

At a certain point you say to the woods, to the sea,

to the mountains, the world, Now I am ready. Now I will stop and be wholly attentive. You empty yourself and wait, listening. After a time you hear it: there is nothing there. There is nothing but those things only, those created objects, discrete, growing or holding, or swaying, being rained on or raining, held, flooding or ebbing, standing, or spread. You feel the world's word as a tension, a hum, a single chorused note everywhere the same. This is it: this hum is the silence. Nature does utter a peep—just this one. The birds and insects, the meadows and swamps and rivers and stones and mountains and clouds: they all do it; they all don't do it. There is a vibrancy to the silence, a suppression, as if someone were gagging the world. But you wait, you give your life's length to listening, and nothing happens. The ice rolls up, the ice rolls back, and still that single note obtains. The tension, or lack of it, is intolerable. The silence is not actually suppression; instead, it is all there is.

V

We are here to witness. There is nothing else to do with those mute materials we do not need. Until Larry teaches his stone to talk, until God changes his mind, or until the pagan gods slip back to their hilltop groves, all we can do with the whole inhuman array is watch it. We can stage our own act on the planet—build our cities on its plains, dam its rivers, plant its topsoils— but our meaningful activity scarcely covers the terrain. We do not use the songbirds, for instance. We do not eat many of them; we cannot befriend them; we cannot persuade them to eat more mosquitoes or plant fewer weed seeds. We can only witness them—whoever they are. If we were not here, they would be songbirds falling in the forest. If we were not here, material events like the passage of seasons would lack even the meager meanings we are able to muster for them. The show would play to an empty house, as do all those falling stars which fall in the daytime. That is why I take walks: to keep an eye on things. And that is why I went to the Galápagos islands.

All this becomes especially clear on the Galápagos islands. The Galápagos islands are just plain here—and little else. They blew up out of the ocean, some plants blew in on them, some animals drifted aboard and evolved weird forms—and there they all are, whoever they are, in full swing. You can go there and watch it happen, and try to figure it out. The Galápagos are a kind of metaphysics laboratory, almost wholly uncluttered by human culture or history. Whatever happens on those bare volcanic rocks happens in full view, whether anyone is watching or not.

What happens there is this, and precious little it is: clouds come and go, and the round of similar seasons; a pig eats a tortoise or doesn't eat a tortoise; Pacific waves fall up and slide back; a lichen expands; night follows day; an albatross dies and dries on a cliff; a cool current upwells from the ocean floor; fishes multiply, flies swarm, stars rise and fall, and diving birds dive. The news, in other words, breaks on the beaches. And taking it all in are the trees. The *palo santo* trees crowd the hillsides like any outdoor audience; they face the lagoons, the lava lowlands, and the shores.

I have some experience of these *palo santo* trees. They interest me as emblems of the muteness of the human stance in relation to all that is not human. I see us all as *palo santo* trees, holy sticks, together watching all that we watch, and growing in silence.

In the Galápagos, it took me a long time to notice the *palo santo* trees. Like everyone else, I specialized in sea lions. My shipmates and I liked the sea lions, and envied their lives. Their joy seemed conscious. They were engaged in full-time play. They were all either fat or dead; there was no halfway. By day they played in the shallows, alone or together, greeting each other and us with great noises of joy, or they took a turn offshore and body-surfed in the breakers, exultant. By night on the sand they lay in each other's flippers and slept. Everyone joked, often, that when he "came back," he would just as soon do it all over again as a sea lion. I concurred. The sea lion game looked unbeatable.

But a year and a half later, I returned to those unpeopled islands. In the interval my attachment to them had shifted, and my memories of them had altered, the way memories do, like particolored pebbles rolled back and forth over a grating, so that after a time those hard bright ones, the ones you thought you would never lose, have vanished, passed through the grating, and only a few big, unexpected ones remain, no longer unnoticed but now selected out for some meaning, large and unknown.

Such were the *palo santo* trees. Before, I had never given them a thought. They were just miles of half-dead trees on the red lava sea cliffs of some deserted islands. They were only a name in a notebook: *"Palo santo*—those strange white trees." Look at the sea lions! Look at the flightless cormorants, the penguins, the iguanas, the sunset! But after eighteen months the wonderful cormorants, penguins, iguanas, sunsets, and even the sea lions, had dropped from my holey heart. I returned to the Galápagos to see the *palo santo* trees.

They are thin, pale, wispy trees. You walk among them on the lowland deserts, where they grow beside the prickly pear. You see them from the water on the steeps that face the sea, hundreds together, small and thin and spread, and so much more pale than their red soils that any black-and-white photograph of them looks like a negative. Their stands look like blasted orchards. At every season they all look newly dead, pale and bare as birches drowned in a beaver pond—for at every season they look leafless, paralyzed, and mute. But in fact, if you look closely, you can see during the rainy months a few meager deciduous leaves here and there on their brittle twigs. And hundreds of lichens always grow on their bark in mute, overlapping explosions which barely enlarge in the course of the decade, lichens pink and orange, lavender, yellow, and green. The *palo santo* trees bear the lichens effortlessly, unconsciously, the way they bear everything. Their multitudes, transparent as line drawings, crowd the cliffsides like whirling dancers, like empty groves, and look out over cliff-wrecked breakers toward more unpeopled islands, with their freakish lizards and birds, toward the grieving lagoons and the bays where the sea lions wander, and beyond to the clamoring seas.

Now I no longer concurred with my shipmates' joke; I no longer wanted to "come back" as a sea lion. For I thought, and I still think, that if I came back to life in the sunlight where everything changes, I would like to come back as a *palo santo* tree, one of thousands on a cliffside on those godforsaken islands, where a million events occur among the witless, where a splash of rain may drop on a yellow iguana the size of a dachshund, and ten minutes later the iguana may blink. I would like to come back as a *palo santo* tree on the weather side of an island, so that I could be, myself, a perfect witness, and look, mute, and wave my arms.

VI

The silence is all there is. It is the alpha and the omega. It is God's brooding over the face of the waters; it is the blended note of the ten thousand things, the whine of wings. You take a step in the right direction to pray to this silence, and even to address the prayer to "World." Distinctions blur. Quit your tents. Pray without ceasing.

On a Hill Far Away

IN VIRGINIA, late one January afternoon while I had a leg of lamb in the oven, I took a short walk. The idea was to exercise my limbs and rest my mind, but these things rarely work out as I plan.

It was sunset by the time I crossed Tinker Creek by hopping from stone to stone and inching up a fallen tree trunk to the bank. On the far side of the creek I followed a barbed-wire fence through steers' pasture and up to a high grassy hill. I'd never been there before. From the hill the distant creek looked still and loaded with sky.

On the hilltop, just across the barbed-wire fence, were three outbuildings: a fenced horse barn, around which a dun mare and a new foal were nervously clattering; a cyclone-fenced dog pen with a barking shepherd and a barking bird dog; and a frame toolshed under whose weedy eaves a little boy was pretending to write with a stone.

The little boy didn't see me. He looked to be about eight, thin, wearing a brown corduroy jacket with darker brown pile on the collar and a matching beaked corduroy cap with big earflaps. He alternated between pretending to write big letters on the toolshed wall and fooling with the dogs from outside their pen. The dogs were going crazy at their fence because of me, and I wondered why the boy didn't turn around; he must be too little to know much about dogs. When he did see me, by accident, his eyebrows shot up. I smiled and hollered and he came over to the barbed wire.

We watched the horses. "How old's the foal?" I asked him. The golden foal looked like a test model in a patent office—jerky, its eyes not set quite right, a marvel. It ran to keep from falling.

"That one is just one. You'd have to say he was *one*. . . ."

Boy, I thought. I sure don't know anything about horses.

". . . he was just *born* six days ago."

The foal wanted to approach. Every time it looked at us, the mare ran interference and edged the foal away.

The boy and I talked over the barbed wire. The dogs' names were Barney and Duke. "Luke?" I said. The boy was shocked. "Duke," he said. He was formal and articulate; he spoke in whole sentences, choosing his words. "I haven't yet settled on a name for the foal, although Father says he is mine." When he spoke this way, he gazed up at me through meeting eyebrows. His dark lips made a projecting circle. He looked like a nineteenth-century cartoon of an Earnest Child. This kid is a fraud, I thought. Who calls his father "Father"? But at other times his face would loosen; I could see then that the accustomed gesture of his lips resembled that of a person trying not to cry. Or he would smile, or look away shyly, like now: "Actually, I've been considering the name Marky Sparky."

"Marky Sparky," I repeated, with as much warmth as I could muster. The sun was down. What was I doing chatting with a little kid? Wasn't there something I should be reading?

Then he paused. He looked miserably at his shoetops, and I looked at his brown corduroy cap. Suddenly the cap lifted, and the little face said in a rush, "Do you know the Lord as your personal savior?"

"Not only that," I said, "I know your mother."

It all came together. She had asked me the same question.

Until then I had not connected this land, these horses, and this little boy with the woman in the big house at the top of the hill, the house I'd approached from the other direction, to ask permission to walk the land. That was about a year ago. There had been a very long driveway from the highway on the other side of the hill. The driveway made a circle in front of the house, and in the circle stood an eight-foot aluminum cross with a sign underneath it reading CHRIST THE LORD IS OUR SALVATION. Spotlights in the circle's honeysuckle were trained up at the cross and the sign. I rang the bell.

The woman was very nervous. She was dark, pretty,

hard, with the same trembling lashes as the boy. She wore a black dress and one brush roller in the front of her hair. She did not ask me in.

My explanation of myself confused her, but she gave permission. Yes, I could walk their property. (She did not add, as others have, "But I don't want no kids in here roughhousing.") She did not let me go; she was worried about something else. She worked her hands. I waited on the other side of the screen door until she came out with it:

"Do you know the Lord as your personal savior?"

My heart went out to her. No wonder she had been so nervous. She must have to ask this of everyone, absolutely everyone, she meets. That is Christian witness. It makes sense, given its premises. I wanted to make her as happy as possible, reward her courage, and run.

She was stunned that I knew the Lord, and clearly uncertain whether we were referring to the same third party. But she had done her bit, bumped over the hump, and now she could relax. She told me about her church, her face brightening. She was part of the Reverend Jerry Falwell's congregation. He is the powerful evangelist in Lynchburg, Virginia, who has recently taken to politics. She drove, I inferred, 120 miles round trip to go to church. While I waited behind the screen door she fetched pamphlets, each a different color. I thanked her kindly; I read them later. The one on the Holy Spirit I thought was good.

So this was her son. She had done a good job. He was a nice little kid. He was glad now his required speech was over; he was glad that I was talking easily, telling about meeting his mother. That I had met her seemed to authenticate me to him and dissolve some wariness.

The wind that follows sunset was blowing from the western ridge, across our hill and down. There had been ice in the creek. The boy moved closer to the barbed-wire fence; he jammed his fists in his pockets. Whenever I smiled or laughed he looked at me disbelieving, and lifted his eyes from beneath his cap's bill again and again to my face.

He never played at the creek, he said. Because he might be down there, and Father might come home not knowing he was there, and let all the horses out, and the horses would trample him. I had noticed that he quailed whenever the mare in her pen jerked his way.

Also there were snakes down there—water moccasins, he said. He seemed tired, old even, weary with longings, solemn. Caution passes for wisdom around here, and this kid knew all the pitfalls. In fact, there are no water moccasins this far north, except out on the coast, but there are some copperheads; I let it go. "They won't hurt you," I said. "I play at the creek," I said. "Lots." How old are you? Eight? Nine? How could you not play at the creek? Or: Why am I trying to force this child to play at the creek? What do I do there alone that he'd want to do? What do I do there at all?

The distant creek looked like ice from the hill, lightless and unmoving. The bare branches of sycamores on its banks met soundlessly. When was spring coming? The sky was purpling. Why would anyone in his right mind play at the creek?

"You're cold," I said to the boy. His lips were blue. He tried to keep his corduroy shoulders against his bare neck. He pretended not to hear. "I have to go," I said. "Do you know how to catch a fish when you haven't got a rod, or a line, or a hook?" He was smiling, warming up for a little dialect, being a kid in a book. He must read a lot. "First, you get you a *stick*. . . ." He explained what sort of stick. "Then you pull you a thread of honeysuckle . . . and if you need you a *hook* . . ."

We talked about fishing. "I've got a roast in the oven," I said. "I've got to go." He had to go too; Father would be home, and the boy had to set the table for dinner. His mother was fasting. I said so long, so long, and turned. He called, "One more thing!" I looked back; he hesitated a second and began loudly, "Did you ever step on a big old snake?"

All right, then. I thanked God for the sisters and friends I had had when I was little; I have not been lonely yet, but it could come at any time. I pulled my jacket collar up as high as I could.

He described stepping on the snake; he rolled his eyes and tried to stir me. "I felt it just . . . *move* under my foot. It was so . . . *slimy*. . . ." I bided my time. His teeth were chattering. "We were walking through the field beneath the cemetery. I called, 'Wait, Father, wait!' I couldn't lift my foot." I wondered what they let him read; he spoke in prose, like *le bourgeois gentilhomme*.

"Gee," I kept saying, "you must have been scared."

"Well, I was *about* knee-deep in honeysuckle."

Oh! That was different. Probably he really *had* stepped on a snake. I would have been plenty scared myself, knee-deep in honeysuckle, but there was no way now to respond to his story all over again, identically but sincerely. Still, it was time to go. It was dark. The mare had nosed her golden foal into the barn. The creek below held a frail color still, the memory of a light that hadn't yet been snuffed.

We parted sadly, over the barbed-wire fence. The boy lowered his enormous, lighted eyes, lifted his shoulders, and went into a classic trudge. He had tried again to keep me there. But I simply had to go. It was dark, it was cold, and I had a roast in the oven, lamb, and I don't like it too well done.

Total Eclipse

IT HAD BEEN LIKE DYING, that sliding down the mountain pass. It had been like the death of someone, irrational, that sliding down the mountain pass and into the region of dread. It was like slipping into fever, or falling down that hole in sleep from which you wake yourself whimpering. We had crossed the mountains that day, and now we were in a strange place—a hotel in central Washington, in a town near Yakima. The eclipse we had traveled here to see would occur early the next morning.

I lay in bed. My husband, Gary, was reading beside me. I lay in bed and looked at the painting on the hotel room wall. It was a print of a detailed and lifelike painting of a smiling clown's head, made out of vegetables. It was a painting of the sort which you do not intend to look at, and which, alas, you never forget. Some tasteless fate presses it upon you; it becomes part of the complex interior junk you carry with you wherever you go. Two years have passed since the total eclipse of which I write. During those years I have forgotten, I assume, a great many things I wanted to remember—but I have not forgotten that clown painting or its lunatic setting in the old hotel.

The clown was bald. Actually, he wore a clown's tight rubber wig, painted white; this stretched over the top of his skull, which was a cabbage. His hair was bunches of baby carrots. Inset in his white clown makeup, and in his cabbage skull, were his small and laughing human eyes. The clown's glance was like the glance of Rembrandt in some of the self-portraits: lively, knowing, deep, and loving. The crinkled shadows around his eyes were string beans. His eyebrows were parsley. Each of his ears was a broad bean. His thin, joyful lips were red chili peppers; between his lips were wet rows of human teeth and a suggestion of a real tongue. The clown print was framed in gilt and glassed.

To put ourselves in the path of the total eclipse, that day we had driven five hours inland from the Washington coast, where we lived. When we tried to cross the Cascades range, an avalanche had blocked the pass.

A slope's worth of snow blocked the road; traffic backed up. Had the avalanche buried any cars that morning? We could not learn. This highway was the only winter road over the mountains. We waited as highway crews bulldozed a passage through the avalanche. With two-by-fours and walls of plyboard, they erected a one-way, roofed tunnel through the avalanche. We drove through the avalanche tunnel, crossed the pass, and descended several thousand feet into central Washington and the broad Yakima valley, about which we knew only that it was orchard country. As we lost altitude, the snows disappeared; our ears popped; the trees changed, and in the trees were strange birds. I watched the landscape innocently, like a fool, like a diver in the rapture of the deep who plays on the bottom while his air runs out.

The hotel lobby was a dark, derelict room, narrow as a corridor, and seemingly without air. We waited on a couch while the manager vanished upstairs to do something unknown to our room. Beside us on an overstuffed chair, absolutely motionless, was a platinum-blond woman in her forties wearing a black silk dress and a strand of pearls. Her long legs were crossed; she supported her head on her fist. At the dim far end of the room, their backs toward us, sat six bald old men in their shirt-sleeves, around a loud television. Two of them seemed asleep. They were drunks. "Number six!" cried the man on television, "Number six!"

On the broad lobby desk, lighted and bubbling, was a ten-gallon aquarium containing one large fish; the fish tilted up and down in its water. Against the long opposite wall sang a live canary in its cage. Beneath the cage, among spilled millet seeds on the carpet, were a decorated child's sand bucket and matching sand shovel.

Now the alarm was set for six. I lay awake remembering an article I had read downstairs in the lobby, in an engineering magazine. The article was about gold mining.

In South Africa, in India, and in South Dakota, the gold mines extend so deeply into the earth's crust that they are hot. The rock walls burn the miners' hands. The companies have to air-condition the mines; if the air conditioners break, the miners die. The elevators in the mine shafts run very slowly, down, and up, so the miners' ears will not pop in their skulls. When the miners return to the surface, their faces are deathly pale.

Early the next morning we checked out. It was February 26, 1979, a Monday morning. We would drive out of town, find a hilltop, watch the eclipse, and then drive back over the mountains and home to the coast. How familiar things are here; how adept we are; how smoothly and professionally we check out! I had forgotten the clown's smiling head and the hotel lobby as if they had never existed. Gary put the car in gear and off we went, as off we have gone to a hundred other adventures.

It was before dawn when we found a highway out of town and drove into the unfamiliar countryside. By the growing light we could see a band of cirrostratus clouds in the sky. Later the rising sun would clear these clouds before the eclipse began. We drove at random until we came to a range of unfenced hills. We pulled off the highway, bundled up, and climbed one of these hills.

II

The hill was five hundred feet high. Long winter-killed grass covered it, as high as our knees. We climbed and rested, sweating in the cold; we passed clumps of bundled people on the hillside who were setting up telescopes and fiddling with cameras. The top of the hill stuck up in the middle of the sky. We tightened our scarves and looked around.

East of us rose another hill like ours. Between the hills, far below, was the highway which threaded south into the valley. This was the Yakima valley; I had never seen it before. It is justly famous for its beauty, like every planted valley. It extended south into the horizon, a distant dream of a valley, a Shangri-la. All its hundreds of low, golden slopes bore orchards. Among the orchards were towns, and roads, and plowed and fallow fields. Through the valley wandered a thin, shining river; from the river extended fine, frozen irrigation ditches. Distance blurred and blued the sight, so that the whole valley looked like a thickness or sediment at the bottom of the sky. Directly behind us was more sky, and empty lowlands blued by distance, and Mount Adams. Mount Adams was an enormous, snow-covered volcanic cone rising flat, like so much scenery.

Now the sun was up. We could not see it; but the sky behind the band of clouds was yellow, and, far down the valley, some hillside orchards had lighted up. More people were parking near the highway and climbing the hills. It was the West. All of us rugged individualists were wearing knit caps and blue nylon parkas. People were climbing the nearby hills and setting up shop in clumps among the dead grasses. It looked as though we had all gathered on hilltops to pray for the world on its last day. It looked as though we had all crawled out of spaceships and were preparing to assault the valley below. It looked as though we were scattered on hilltops at dawn to sacrifice virgins, make rain, set stone stelae in a ring. There was no place out of the wind. The straw grasses banged our legs.

Up in the sky where we stood the air was lusterless yellow. To the west the sky was blue. Now the sun cleared the clouds. We cast rough shadows on the blowing grass; freezing, we waved our arms. Near the sun, the sky was bright and colorless. There was nothing to see.

It began with no ado. It was odd that such a well-advertised public event should have no starting gun, no overture, no introductory speaker. I should have known right then that I was out of my depth. Without pause or preamble, silent as orbits, a piece of the sun went away. We looked at it through welders' goggles. A piece of the sun was missing; in its place we saw empty sky.

I had seen a partial eclipse in 1970. A partial eclipse is very interesting. It bears almost no relation to a total eclipse. Seeing a partial eclipse bears the same relation to seeing a total eclipse as kissing a man does to marrying him, or as flying in an airplane does to falling out of an airplane. Although the one experience precedes the other, it in no way prepares you for it. During a partial eclipse the sky does not darken—not even when 94 percent of the sun is hidden. Nor does the sun, seen colorless through protective devices, seem terribly strange. We have all seen a sliver of light in the sky; we have all seen the crescent moon by day. However, during a partial eclipse the air does indeed get cold, precisely as if someone were standing between you and the fire. And blackbirds do fly back to their roosts. I had seen a partial eclipse before, and here was another.

What you see in an eclipse is entirely different from what you know. It is especially different for those of us whose grasp of astronomy is so frail that, given a flashlight, a grapefruit, two oranges, and fifteen years, we still could not figure out which way to set the clocks for Daylight Saving Time. Usually it is a bit of a trick to keep your knowledge from blinding you. But during an eclipse it is easy. What you see is much more convincing than any wild-eyed theory you may know.

You may read that the moon has something to do with eclipses. I have never seen the moon yet. You do not see the moon. So near the sun, it is as completely invisible as the stars are by day. What you see before your eyes is the sun going through phases. It gets narrower and narrower, as the waning moon does, and, like the ordinary moon, it travels alone in the simple sky. The sky is of course background. It does not appear to eat the sun; it is far behind the sun. The sun simply shaves away; gradually, you see less sun and more sky.

The sky's blue was deepening, but there was no darkness. The sun was a wide crescent, like a segment of tangerine. The wind freshened and blew steadily over the hill. The eastern hill across the highway grew dusky and sharp. The towns and orchards in the valley to the south were dissolving into the blue light. Only the thin river held a trickle of sun.

Now the sky to the west deepened to indigo, a color never seen. A dark sky usually loses color. This was a saturated, deep indigo, up in the air. Stuck up into that unworldly sky was the cone of Mount Adams, and the alpenglow was upon it. The alpenglow is that red light of sunset which holds out on snowy mountaintops long after the valleys and tablelands are dimmed. "Look at Mount Adams," I said, and that was the last sane moment I remember.

I turned back to the sun. It was going. The sun was going, and the world was wrong. The grasses were wrong; they were platinum. Their every detail of stem, head, and blade shone lightless and artificially distinct as an art photographer's platinum print. This color has never been seen on earth. The hues were metallic; their finish was matte. The hillside was a nineteenth-century tinted photograph from which the tints had faded. All the people you see in the photograph, distinct and detailed as their faces look, are now dead. The sky was navy blue. My hands were silver. All the distant hills' grasses were finespun metal which the wind laid down. I was watching a faded color print of a movie filmed in the Middle Ages; I was standing in it, by some mistake. I was standing in a movie of hillside grasses filmed in the Middle Ages. I missed my own century, the people I knew, and the real light of day.

I looked at Gary. He was in the film. Everything was lost. He was a platinum print, a dead artist's version of life. I saw on his skull the darkness of night mixed with the colors of day. My mind was going out; my eyes were receding the way galaxies recede to the rim of space. Gary was light-years away, gesturing inside a circle of darkness, down the wrong end of a telescope. He smiled as if he saw me; the stringy crinkles around his eyes moved. The sight of him, familiar and wrong, was something I was remembering from centuries hence, from the other side of death: yes, *that* is the way he used to look, when we were living. When it was our generation's turn to be alive. I could not hear him; the wind was too loud. Behind him the sun was going. We had all started down a chute of time. At first it was pleasant; now there was no stopping it. Gary was chuting away across space, moving and talking and catching my eye, chuting down the long corridor of separation. The skin on his face moved like thin bronze plating that would peel.

The grass at our feet was wild barley. It was the wild einkorn wheat which grew on the hilly flanks of the Zagros Mountains, above the Euphrates valley, above the valley of the river we called *River*. We harvested the grass with stone sickles, I remember. We found the grasses on the hillsides; we built our shelter beside them and cut them down. That is how he used to look then, that one, moving and living and catching my eye, with the sky so dark behind him, and the wind blowing. God save our life.

From all the hills came screams. A piece of sky beside the crescent sun was detaching. It was a loosened circle of evening sky, suddenly lighted from the back. It was an abrupt black body out of nowhere; it was a flat disk; it was almost over the sun. That is when there were screams. At once this disk of sky slid over the sun like a lid. The sky snapped over the sun like a lens cover. The hatch in the brain slammed. Abruptly it was dark night, on the land and in the sky. In the night sky was a tiny ring of light. The hole where the sun belongs is very small. A thin ring of light marked its place. There was no sound. The eyes dried, the arteries drained, the lungs hushed. There was no world. We were the world's dead people rotating and orbiting around and around, embedded in the planet's crust, while the earth rolled down. Our minds were light-years distant, forgetful of almost everything. Only an extraordinary act of will could recall to us our former, living selves and our contexts in matter and time. We had, it seems, loved the planet and loved our lives, but could no longer remember the way of them. We got the light wrong. In the sky was something that should not be there. In the black sky was a ring of light. It was a thin ring, an old, thin silver wedding band, an old, worn ring. It was an old wedding band in the sky, or a morsel of bone. There were stars. It was all over.

III

It is now that the temptation is strongest to leave these regions. We have seen enough; let's go. Why burn our hands any more than we have to? But two years have passed; the price of gold has risen. I return to the same buried alluvial beds and pick through the strata again.

I saw, early in the morning, the sun diminish against a backdrop of sky. I saw a circular piece of that sky appear, suddenly detached, blackened, and backlighted; from nowhere it came and overlapped the sun. It did not look like the moon. It was enormous and black. If I had not read that it was the moon, I could have seen the sight a hundred times and never thought of the moon once. (If, however, I had not read that it was the moon— if, like most of the world's people throughout time, I had simply glanced up and seen this thing—then I doubtless would not have speculated much, but would have, like Emperor Louis of Bavaria in 840, simply died of fright on the spot.) It did not look like a dragon, although it looked more like a dragon than the moon. It looked like a lens cover, or the lid of a pot. It materialized out of thin air—black, and flat, and sliding, outlined in flame.

Seeing this black body was like seeing a mushroom cloud. The heart screeched. The meaning of the sight overwhelmed its fascination. It obliterated meaning itself. If you were to glance out one day and see a row of mushroom clouds rising on the horizon, you would know at once that what you were seeing, remarkable as it was, was intrinsically not worth remarking. No use running to tell anyone. Significant as it was, it did not matter a whit. For what is significance? It is significance for people. No people, no significance. This is all I have to tell you.

In the deeps are the violence and terror of which psychology has warned us. But if you ride these monsters deeper down, if you drop with them farther over the world's rim, you find what our sciences cannot locate or name, the substrate, the ocean or matrix or ether which buoys the rest, which gives goodness its power for good, and evil its power for evil, the unified field: our complex and inexplicable caring for each other, and for our life together here. This is given. It is not learned.

The world which lay under darkness and stillness following the closing of the lid was not the world we know. The event was over. Its devastation lay round about us. The clamoring mind and heart stilled, almost indifferent, certainly disembodied, frail, and exhausted. The hills were hushed, obliterated. Up in the sky, like a crater from some distant cataclysm, was a hollow ring.

You have seen photographs of the sun taken during a total eclipse. The corona fills the print. All of those photographs were taken through telescopes. The lenses of telescopes and cameras can no more cover the breadth and scale of the visual array than language can cover the breadth and simultaneity of internal experience. Lenses enlarge the sight, omit its context, and make of it a pretty and sensible picture, like something on a Christmas card. I assure you, if you send any shepherds a Christmas card on which is printed a three-by-three photograph of the angel of the Lord, the glory of the Lord, and a multitude of the heavenly host, they will not be sore afraid. More fearsome things can come in envelopes. More moving photographs than those of the sun's corona can appear in magazines. But I pray you will never see anything more awful in the sky.

You see the wide world swaddled in darkness; you see a vast breadth of hilly land, and an enormous, distant, blackened valley; you see towns' lights, a river's path, and blurred portions of your hat and scarf; you see your husband's face looking like an early black-and-white film; and you see a sprawl of black sky and blue sky together, with unfamiliar stars in it, some barely visible bands of cloud, and over there, a small white ring. The

ring is as small as one goose in a flock of migrating geese—
if you happen to notice a flock of migrating geese. It is
one 360th part of the visible sky. The sun we see is
less than half the diameter of a dime held at arm's length.

The Crab Nebula, in the constellation Taurus, looks,
through binoculars, like a smoke ring. It is a star in the
process of exploding. Light from its explosion first
reached the earth in 1054; it was a supernova then, and
so bright it shone in the daytime. Now it is not so bright,
but it is still exploding. It expands at the rate of seventy
million miles a day. It is interesting to look through binoculars at something expanding seventy million miles a
day. It does not budge. Its apparent size does not increase.
Photographs of the Crab Nebula taken fifteen years ago
seem identical to photographs of it taken yesterday. Some
lichens are similar. Botanists have measured some ordinary lichens twice, at fifty-year intervals, without detect-
ing any growth at all. And yet their cells divide; they
live.

The small ring of light was like these things—like a
ridiculous lichen up in the sky, like a perfectly still explosion 4,200 light-years away: it was interesting, and
lovely, and in witless motion, and it had nothing to do
with anything.

It had nothing to do with anything. The sun was too
small, and too cold, and too far away, to keep the world
alive. The white ring was not enough. It was feeble and
worthless. It was as useless as a memory; it was as off
kilter and hollow and wretched as a memory.

When you try your hardest to recall someone's face,
or the look of a place, you see in your mind's eye some

vague and terrible sight such as this. It is dark; it is insubstantial; it is all wrong.

The white ring and the saturated darkness made the earth and the sky look as they must look in the memories of the careless dead. What I saw, what I seemed to be standing in, was all the wrecked light that the memories of the dead could shed upon the living world. We had all died in our boots on the hilltops of Yakima, and were alone in eternity. Empty space stoppered our eyes and mouths; we cared for nothing. We remembered our living days wrong. With great effort we had remembered some sort of circular light in the sky—but only the outline. Oh, and then the orchard trees withered, the ground froze, the glaciers slid down the valleys and overlapped the towns. If there had ever been people on earth, nobody knew it. The dead had forgotten those they had loved. The dead were parted one from the other and could no longer remember the faces and lands they had loved in the light. They seemed to stand on darkened hilltops, looking down.

IV

We teach our children one thing only, as we were taught: to wake up. We teach our children to look alive there, to join by words and activities the life of human culture on the planet's crust. As adults we are almost all adept at waking up. We have so mastered the transition we have forgotten we ever learned it. Yet it is a transition we make a hundred times a day, as, like so many will-less dolphins, we plunge and surface, lapse and emerge. We live half our waking lives and all of our sleeping lives in some private, useless, and insensible waters we never mention or recall. Useless, I say. Valueless, I might add—until someone hauls their wealth up to the surface and into the wide-awake city, in a form that people can use.

I do not know how we got to the restaurant. Like Roethke, "I take my waking slow." Gradually I seemed more or less alive, and already forgetful. It was now almost nine in the morning. It was the day of a solar eclipse in central Washington, and a fine adventure for everyone. The sky was clear; there was a fresh breeze out of the north.

The restaurant was a roadside place with tables and booths. The other eclipse-watchers were there. From our booth we could see their cars' California license plates, their University of Washington parking stickers. Inside the restaurant we were all eating eggs or waffles; people were fairly shouting and exchanging enthusiasms, like fans after a World Series game. Did you see . . . ? Did you see . . . ? Then somebody said something which knocked me for a loop.

A college student, a boy in a blue parka who carried a Hasselblad, said to us, "Did you see that little white ring? It looked like a Life Saver. It looked like a Life Saver up in the sky."

And so it did. The boy spoke well. He was a walking alarm clock. I myself had at that time no access to such a word. He could write a sentence, and I could not. I grabbed that Life Saver and rode it to the surface. And I had to laugh. I had been dumbstruck on the Euphrates River, I had been dead and gone and grieving, all over the sight of something which, if you could claw your way up to that level, you would grant looked very much like a Life Saver. It was good to be back among people so clever; it was good to have all the world's words at the mind's disposal, so the mind could begin its task. All those things for which we have no words are lost. The mind—the culture—has two little tools, grammar and lexicon: a decorated sand bucket and a matching shovel. With these we bluster about the continents and do all the world's work. With these we try to save our very lives.

There are a few more things to tell from this level, the level of the restaurant. One is the old joke about breakfast. "It can never be satisfied, the mind, never." Wallace Stevens wrote that, and in the long run he was right. The mind wants to live forever, or to learn a very good reason why not. The mind wants the world to return its love, or its awareness; the mind wants to know all the world, and all eternity, and God. The mind's sidekick, however, will settle for two eggs over easy.

The dear, stupid body is as easily satisfied as a spaniel. And, incredibly, the simple spaniel can lure the brawling mind to its dish. It is everlastingly funny that the proud, metaphysically ambitious, clamoring mind will hush if you give it an egg.

Further: while the mind reels in deep space, while the mind grieves or fears or exults, the workaday senses, in ignorance or idiocy, like so many computer terminals printing out market prices while the world blows up, still transcribe their little data and transmit them to the warehouse in the skull. Later, under the tranquilizing influence of fried eggs, the mind can sort through this data. The restaurant was a halfway house, a decompression chamber. There I remembered a few things more.

The deepest, and most terrifying, was this: I have said that I heard screams. (I have since read that screaming, with hysteria, is a common reaction even to expected total eclipses.) People on all the hillsides, including, I think, myself, screamed when the black body of the moon detached from the sky and rolled over the sun. But something else was happening at that same instant, and it was this, I believe, which made us scream.

The second before the sun went out we saw a wall of dark shadow come speeding at us. We no sooner saw it than it was upon us, like thunder. It roared up the valley. It slammed our hill and knocked us out. It was the monstrous swift shadow cone of the moon. I have since read that this wave of shadow moves 1,800 miles an hour. Language can give no sense of this sort of speed—1,800 miles an hour. It was 195 miles wide. No end was in sight—you saw only the edge. It rolled at you across the land at 1,800 miles an hour, hauling darkness like plague behind it. Seeing it, and knowing it was coming straight for you, was like feeling a slug of anesthetic shoot up your arm. If you think very fast, you may have time to think, "Soon it will hit my brain." You can feel the deadness race up your arm; you can feel the appalling, inhuman speed of your own blood. We saw the wall of shadow coming, and screamed before it hit.

This was the universe about which we have read so much and never before felt: the universe as a clockwork of loose spheres flung at stupefying, unauthorized speeds. How could anything moving so fast not crash, not veer from its orbit amok like a car out of control on a turn? Less than two minutes later, when the sun emerged, the trailing edge of the shadow cone sped away. It coursed down our hill and raced eastward over the plain, faster than the eye could believe; it swept over the plain and dropped over the planet's rim in a twinkling. It had clobbered us, and now it roared away. We blinked in the light. It was as though an enormous, loping god in the sky had reached down and slapped the earth's face.

Something else, something more ordinary, came back to me along about the third cup of coffee. During the moments of totality, it was so dark that drivers on the highway below turned on their cars' headlights. We could see the highway's route as a strand of lights. It was bumper-to-bumper down there. It was eight-fifteen in the morning, Monday morning, and people were driving into Yakima to work. That it was as dark as night, and eerie as hell, an hour after dawn, apparently meant that in order to *see* to drive to work, people had to use their headlights. Four or five cars pulled off the road. The rest, in a line at least five miles long, drove to town. The highway ran between hills; the people could not have seen any of the eclipsed sun at all. Yakima will have another total eclipse in 2086. Perhaps, in 2086, businesses will give their employees an hour off.

From the restaurant we drove back to the coast. The highway crossing the Cascades range was open. We drove over the mountain like old pros. We joined our places on the planet's thin crust; it held. For the time being, we were home free.

Early that morning at six, when we had checked out, the six bald men were sitting on folding chairs in the dim hotel lobby. The television was on. Most of them were awake. You might drown in your own spittle, God knows, at any time; you might wake up dead in a small hotel, a cabbage head watching TV while snows pile up in the passes, watching TV while the chili peppers smile and the moon passes over the sun and nothing changes and nothing is learned because you have lost your bucket and shovel and no longer care. What if you regain the surface and open your sack and find, instead of treasure, a beast which jumps at you? Or you may not come back at all. The winches may jam, the scaffolding buckle, the air conditioning collapse. You may glance up one day and see by your headlamp the canary keeled over in its cage. You may reach into a cranny for pearls and touch a moray eel. You yank on your rope; it is too late.

Apparently people share a sense of these hazards, for when the total eclipse ended, an odd thing happened.

When the sun appeared as a blinding bead on the ring's side, the eclipse was over. The black lens cover appeared again, backlighted, and slid away. At once the yellow light made the sky blue again; the black lid dissolved and vanished. The real world began there. I remember now: we all hurried away. We were born and bored at a stroke. We rushed down the hill. We found our car; we saw the other people streaming down the hillsides; we joined the highway traffic and drove away.

We never looked back. It was a general vamoose, and an odd one, for when we left the hill, the sun was still partially eclipsed—a sight rare enough, and one which, in itself, we would probably have driven five hours to see. But enough is enough. One turns at last even from glory itself with a sigh of relief. From the depths of mystery, and even from the heights of splendor, we bounce back and hurry for the latitudes of home.

Lenses

You get used to looking through lenses; it is an acquired skill. When you first look through binoculars, for instance, you can't see a thing. You look at the inside of the barrel; you blink and watch your eyelashes; you play with the focus knob till one eye is purblind.

The microscope is even worse. You are supposed to keep both eyes open as you look through its single eyepiece. I spent my childhood in Pittsburgh trying to master this trick: seeing through one eye, with both eyes open. The microscope also teaches you to move your hands wrong, to shove the glass slide to the right if you are following a creature who is swimming off to the left— as if you were operating a tiller, or backing a trailer, or performing any other of those paradoxical maneuvers which require either sure instincts or a grasp of elementary physics, neither of which I possess.

A child's microscope set comes with a little five-watt lamp. You place this dim light in front of the microscope's mirror; the mirror bounces the light up through the slide, through the magnifying lenses, and into your eye. The only reason you do not see everything in silhouette is that microscopic things are so small they are translucent. The animals and plants in a drop of pond water pass light like pale stained glass; they seem so soaked in water and light that their opacity has leached away.

The translucent strands of algae you see under a microscope—Spirogyra, Oscillatoria, Cladophora—move of their own accord, no one knows how or why. You watch these swaying yellow, green, and brown strands of algae half mesmerized; you sink into the microscope's field forgetful, oblivious, as if it were all a dream of your deepest brain. Occasionally a zippy rotifer comes barreling through, black and white, and in a tremendous hurry.

My rotifers and daphniae and amoebae were in an especially tremendous hurry because they were drying up. I burnt out or broke my little five-watt bulb right away. To replace it, I rigged an old table lamp laid on its side; the table lamp carried a seventy-five-watt bulb. I was about twelve, immortal and invulnerable, and did not know what I was doing; neither did anyone else. My parents let me set up my laboratory in the basement, where they wouldn't have to smell the urine I collected in test tubes and kept in the vain hope it would grow something horrible. So in full, solitary ignorance I spent evenings in the basement staring into a seventy-five-watt bulb magnified three hundred times and focused into my eye. It is a wonder I can see at all. My eyeball itself would start drying up; I blinked and blinked.

But the pond water creatures fared worse. I dropped them on a slide, floated a cover slip over them, and laid the slide on the microscope's stage, which the seventy-five-watt bulb had heated like a grill. At once the drop of pond water started to evaporate. Its edges shrank. The creatures swam among algae in a diminishing pool. I liked this part. The heat worked for me as a centrifuge, to concentrate the biomass. I had about five minutes to watch the members of a very dense population, excited by the heat, go about their business until—as I fancied sadly—they all caught on to their situation and started making out wills.

I was, then, not only watching the much-vaunted wonders in a drop of pond water; I was also, with mingled sadism and sympathy, setting up a limitless series of apocalypses. I set up and staged hundreds of ends-of-the-world and watched, enthralled, as they played themselves out. Over and over again, the last trump sounded, the final scroll unrolled, and the known world drained, dried, and vanished. When all the creatures lay motionless, boiled and fried in the positions they had when the last of their water dried completely, I washed the slide in the sink and started over with a fresh drop. How I loved that deep, wet world where the colored algae waved in the water and the rotifers swam!

But oddly, this is a story about swans. It is not even a story; it is a description of swans. This description of swans includes the sky over a pond, a pair of binoculars, and a mortal adult who had long since moved out of the Pittsburgh basement.

In the Roanoke valley of Virginia, rimmed by the Blue Ridge Mountains to the east and the Allegheny Mountains to the west, is a little semi-agricultural area called Daleville. In Daleville, set among fallow fields and wooded ridges, is Daleville Pond. It is a big pond, maybe ten acres; it holds a lot of sky. I used to haunt the place because I loved it; I still do. In winter it had that airy scruffiness of deciduous lands; you greet the daylight and the open space, and spend the evening picking burrs out of your pants.

One Valentine's Day, in the afternoon, I was crouched among dried reeds at the edge of Daleville Pond. Across the pond from where I crouched was a low forested mountain ridge. In every other direction I saw only sky, sky crossed by the reeds which blew before my face whichever way I turned.

I was looking through binoculars at a pair of whistling swans. Whistling swans! It is impossible to say how excited I was to see whistling swans in Daleville, Virginia. The two were a pair, mated for life, migrating north and west from the Atlantic coast to the high arctic. They had paused to feed at Daleville Pond. I had flushed them, and now they were flying and circling the pond. I crouched in the reeds so they would not be afraid to come back to the water.

Through binoculars I followed the swans, swinging where they flew. All their feathers were white; their eyes were black. Their wingspan was six feet; they were bigger than I was. They flew in unison, one behind the other;

they made pass after pass at the pond. I watched them change from white swans in front of the mountain to black swans in front of the sky. In clockwise ellipses they flew, necks long and relaxed, alternately beating their wide wings and gliding.

As I rotated on my heels to keep the black frame of the lenses around them, I lost all sense of space. If I lowered the binoculars I was always amazed to learn in which direction I faced—dazed, the way you emerge awed from a movie and try to reconstruct, bit by bit, a real world, in order to discover where in it you might have parked the car.

I lived in that circle of light, in great speed and utter silence. When the swans passed before the sun they were distant—two black threads, two live stitches. But they kept coming, smoothly, and the sky deepened to blue behind them and they took on light. They gathered dimension as they neared, and I could see their ardent, straining eyes. Then I could hear the brittle blur of their wings, the blur which faded as they circled on, and the sky brightened to yellow behind them and the swans flattened and darkened and diminished as they flew. Once I lost them behind the mountain ridge; when they emerged they were flying suddenly very high, and it was like music changing key.

I was lost. The reeds in front of me, swaying and out of focus in the binoculars' circular field, were translucent. The reeds were strands of color passing light like cells in water. They were those yellow and green and brown strands of pond algae I had watched so long in a light-soaked field. My eyes burned; I was watching algae wave in a shrinking drop; they crossed each other and parted wetly. And suddenly into the field swam two whistling swans, two tiny whistling swans. They swam as fast as rotifers: two whistling swans, infinitesimal, beating their tiny wet wings, perfectly formed.

Life on the Rocks:
The Galápagos

I

FIRST THERE WAS NOTHING, and although you know with your reason that nothing is nothing, it is easier to visualize it as a limitless slosh of sea—say, the Pacific. Then energy contracted into matter, and although you know that even an invisible gas is matter, it is easier to visualize it as a massive squeeze of volcanic lava spattered inchoate from the secret pit of the ocean and hardening mute and intractable on nothing's lapping shore—like a series of islands, an archipelago. Like: the Galápagos. Then a softer strain of matter began to twitch. It was a kind of shaped water; it flowed, hardening here and there at its tips.

There were blue-green algae; there were tortoises.

The ice rolled up, the ice rolled back, and I knelt on a plain of lava boulders in the islands called Galápagos, stroking a giant tortoise's neck. The tortoise closed its eyes and stretched its neck to its greatest height and vulnerability. I rubbed that neck, and when I pulled away my hand, my palm was green with a slick of single-celled algae. I stared at the algae, and at the tortoise, the way you stare at any life on a lava flow, and thought: Well—here we all are.

Being here is being here on the rocks. These Galapagonian rocks, one of them seventy-five miles long, have dried under the equatorial sun between five and six hundred miles west of the South American continent; they lie at the latitude of the Republic of Ecuador, to which they belong.

There is a way a small island rises from the ocean affronting all reason. It is a chunk of chaos pounded into visibility *ex nihilo*: here rough, here smooth, shaped just so by a matrix of physical necessities too weird to contemplate, here instead of there, here instead of not at all. It is a fantastic utterance, as though I were to open my mouth and emit a French horn, or a vase, or a knob of tellurium. It smacks of folly, of first causes.

I think of the island called Daphnecita, little Daphne, on which I never set foot. It's in half of my few photographs, though, because it obsessed me: a dome of gray lava like a pitted loaf, the size of the Plaza Hotel, glazed with guano and crawling with red-orange crabs. Sometimes I attributed to this island's cliff face a surly, infantile consciousness, as though it were sulking in the silent moment after it had just shouted, to the sea and the sky, "I didn't ask to be born." Or sometimes it aged to a raging adolescent, a kid who's just learned that the game is fixed, demanding, "What did you have me for, if you're just going to push me around?" Daphnecita: again, a wise old island, mute, leading the life of pure creaturehood open to any antelope or saint. After you've blown the ocean sky-high, what's there to say? What if we the people had the sense or grace to live as cooled islands in an archipelago live, with dignity, passion, and no comment?

It is worth flying to Guayaquil, Ecuador, and then to Baltra in the Galápagos just to see the rocks. But these rocks are animal gardens. They are home to a Hieronymus Bosch assortment of windblown, stowaway, castaway, flotsam, and shipwrecked creatures. Most exist nowhere else on earth. These reptiles and insects, small mammals and birds, evolved unmolested on the various islands on which they were cast into unique species adapted to the boulder-wrecked shores, the cactus deserts of the lowlands, or the elevated jungles of the large islands' interiors. You come for the animals. You come to see the curious shapes soft proteins can take, to impress yourself with their reality, and to greet them.

You walk among clattering four-foot marine iguanas heaped on the shore lava, and on each other, like slag. You swim with penguins; you watch flightless cormorants dance beside you, ignoring you, waving the black nubs of their useless wings. Here are nesting blue-footed boobies, real birds with real feathers, whose legs and feet are nevertheless patently fake, manufactured by Mattel.

The tortoises are big as stoves. The enormous land iguanas at your feet change color in the sunlight, from gold to blotchy red as you watch.

There is always some creature going about its beautiful business. I missed the boat back to my ship, and was left behind momentarily on uninhabited South Plaza island, because I was watching the Audubon's shearwaters. These dark pelagic birds flick along pleated seas in stitching flocks, flailing their wings rapidly—because if they don't, they'll stall. A shearwater must fly fast, or not at all. Consequently it has evolved two nice behaviors which serve to bring it into its nest alive. The nest is a shearwater-sized hole in the lava cliff. The shearwater circles over the water, ranging out from the nest a quarter of a mile, and veers gradually toward the cliff, making passes at its nest. If the flight angle is precisely right, the bird will fold its wings at the hole's entrance and stall directly onto its floor. The angle is perhaps seldom right, however; one shearwater I watched made a dozen suicidal-looking passes before it vanished into a chink. The other behavior is spectacular. It involves choosing the nest hole in a site below a prominent rock with a downward-angled face. The shearwater comes careering in at full tilt, claps its wings, stalls itself into the rock, and the rock, acting as a backboard, banks it home.

The animals are tame. They have not been persecuted, and show no fear of man. You pass among them as though you were wind, spindrift, sunlight, leaves. The songbirds are tame. On Hood Island I sat beside a nesting waved albatross while a mockingbird scratched in my hair, another mockingbird jabbed at my fingernail, and a third mockingbird made an exquisite progression of pokes at my bare feet up the long series of eyelets in my basketball shoes. The marine iguanas are tame. One settler, Carl Angermeyer, built his house on the site of a marine iguana colony. The gray iguanas, instead of moving out, moved up on the roof, which is corrugated steel. Twice daily on the patio, Angermeyer feeds them a mixture of boiled rice and tuna fish from a plastic basin. Their names are all, unaccountably, Annie. Angermeyer beats on the basin with a long-handled spoon, calling, "Here AnnieAnnie-AnnieAnnie"—and the spiny reptiles, fifty or sixty strong, click along the steel roof, finger their way down the lava boulder and mortar walls, and swarm round his bare legs to elbow into the basin and be elbowed out again smeared with a mash of boiled rice on their bellies and on their protuberant, black, plated lips.

The wild hawk is tame. The Galápagos hawk is related to North America's Swainson's hawk; I have read that if you take pains, you can walk up and pat it. I never tried. We people don't walk up and pat each other; enough is enough. The animals' critical distance and mine tended to coincide, so we could enjoy an easy sociability without threat of violence or unwonted intimacy. The hawk, which is not notably sociable, nevertheless endures even a blundering approach, and is apparently as content to perch on a scrub tree at your shoulder as anyplace else.

In the Galápagos, even the flies are tame. Although most of the land is Ecuadorian national park, and as such rigidly protected, I confess I gave the evolutionary ball an offsides shove by dispatching every fly that bit me, marveling the while at its pristine ignorance, its blithe failure to register a flight trigger at the sweep of my descending hand—an insouciance that was almost, but not quite, disarming. After you kill a fly, you pick it up and feed it to a lava lizard, a bright-throated four-inch lizard that scavenges everywhere in the arid lowlands. And you walk on, passing among the innocent mobs on every rock hillside; or you sit, and they come to you.

We are strangers and sojourners, soft dots on the rocks. You have walked along the strand and seen where birds have landed, walked, and flown; their tracks begin in sand, and go, and suddenly end. Our tracks do that: but we go down. And stay down. While we're here, during the seasons our tents are pitched in the light, we pass among each other crying "greetings" in a thousand tongues, and "welcome," and "good-bye." Inhabitants of uncrowded colonies tend to offer the stranger famously warm hospitality—and such are the Galápagos sea lions. Theirs is the greeting the first creatures must have given Adam—a hero's welcome, a universal and undeserved huzzah. Go, and be greeted by sea lions.

I was sitting with ship's naturalist Soames Summerhays on a sand beach under cliffs on uninhabited Hood Island. The white beach was a havoc of lava boulders black as clinkers, sleek with spray, and lambent as brass in the sinking sun. To our left a dozen sea lions were body-surfing in the long green combers that rose, translucent, half a mile offshore. When the combers broke, the shoreline boulders rolled. I could feel the roar in the rough rock on which I sat; I could hear the grate inside each long backsweeping sea, the rumble of a rolled million rocks muffled in splashes and the seethe before the next wave's heave.

To our right, a sea lion slipped from the ocean. It was a young bull; in another few years he would be dangerous, bellowing at intruders and biting off great dirty chunks of the ones he caught. Now this young bull, which weighed maybe 120 pounds, sprawled silhouetted in the late light, slick as a drop of quicksilver, his glistening whiskers radii of gold like any crown. He hauled his packed bulk toward us up the long beach; he flung himself with an enormous surge of fur-clad muscle onto the boulder where I sat. "Soames," I said—very quietly, "he's here because *we're* here, isn't he?" The naturalist nodded. I felt water drip on my elbow behind me, then the fragile scrape of whiskers, and finally the wet warmth and weight of a muzzle, as the creature settled to sleep on my arm. I was catching on to sea lions.

Walk into the water. Instantly sea lions surround you, even if none has been in sight. To say that they come to play with you is not especially anthropomorphic. Animals play. The bull sea lions are off patrolling their territorial shores; these are the cows and young, which range freely. A five-foot sea lion peers intently into your face, then urges her muzzle gently against your underwater mask and searches your eyes without blinking. Next she rolls upside down and slides along the length of your floating body, rolls again, and casts a long glance back at your eyes. You are, I believe, supposed to follow, and think up something clever in return. You can play games with sea lions in the water using shells or bits of leaf, if you are willing. You can spin on your vertical axis and a sea lion will swim circles around you, keeping her face always six inches from yours, as though she were tethered. You can make a game of touching their back flippers, say, and the sea lions will understand at once; somersaulting conveniently before your clumsy hands, they will give you an excellent field of back flippers.

And when you leave the water, they follow. They don't want you to go. They porpoise to the shore, popping their heads up when they lose you and casting about, then speeding to your side and emitting a choked series of vocal notes. If you won't relent, they disappear, barking; but if you sit on the beach with so much as a foot in the water, two or three will station with you, floating on their backs and saying, Urr.

Few people come to the Galápagos. Buccaneers used to anchor in the bays to avoid pursuit, to rest, and to lighter on fresh water. The world's whaling ships stopped here as well, to glut their holds with fresh meat in the form of giant tortoises. The whalers used to let the tortoises bang around on deck for a few days to empty their guts; then they stacked them below on their backs to live—if you call that living—without food or water for a year. When they wanted fresh meat, they killed one.

Early inhabitants of the islands were a desiccated assortment of grouches, cranks, and ships' deserters. These hardies shot, poisoned, and enslaved each other off, leaving behind a fecund gang of feral goats, cats, dogs, and pigs whose descendants skulk in the sloping jungles and take their tortoise hatchlings neat. Now scientists at the

Charles Darwin Research Station, on the island of Santa Cruz, rear the tortoise hatchlings for several years until their shells are tough enough to resist the crunch; then they release them in the wilds of their respective islands. Today, some few thousand people live on three of the islands; settlers from Ecuador, Norway, Germany, and France make a livestock or pineapple living from the rich volcanic soils. The settlers themselves seem to embody a high degree of courteous and conscious humanity, perhaps because of their relative isolation.

On the island of Santa Cruz, eleven fellow passengers and I climb in an open truck up the Galápagos' longest road; we shift to horses, burros, and mules, and visit the lonely farm of Alf Kastdalen. He came to the islands as a child with his immigrant parents from Norway. Now a broad, blond man in his late forties with children of his own, he lives in an isolated house of finished timbers imported from the mainland, on four hundred acres he claimed from the jungle by hand. He raises cattle. He walks us round part of his farm, smiling expansively and meeting our chatter with a willing, open gaze and kind words. The pasture looks like any pasture—but the rocks under the grass are round lava ankle-breakers, the copses are a tangle of thorny bamboo and bromeliads, and the bordering trees dripping in epiphytes are breadfruit, papaya, avocado, and orange.

Kastdalen's isolated house is heaped with books in three languages. He knows animal husbandry; he also knows botany and zoology. He feeds us soup, chicken worth chewing for, green *naranjilla* juice, noodles, pork in big chunks, marinated mixed vegetables, rice, and bowl after bowl of bright mixed fruits.

And his isolated Norwegian mother sees us off; our beasts are ready. We will ride down the mud forest track to the truck at the Ecuadorian settlement, down the long road to the boat, and across the bay to the ship. I lean down to catch her words. She is gazing at me with enormous warmth. "Your hair," she says softly. I am blond. *Adiós.*

II

Charles Darwin came to the Galápagos in 1835, on the *Beagle;* he was twenty-six. He threw the marine iguanas as far as he could into the water; he rode the tortoises and sampled their meat. He noticed that the tortoises' carapaces varied wildly from island to island; so also did the forms of various mockingbirds. He made collections. Nine years later he wrote in a letter, "I am almost convinced (quite contrary to the opinion I started with) that species are not (it is like confessing a murder) immutable." In 1859 he published *On the Origin of Species,* and in 1871 *The Descent of Man.* It is fashionable now to disparage Darwin's originality; not even the surliest of his detractors, however, faults his painstaking methods or denies his impact.

Darwinism today is more properly called neo-Darwinism. It is organic evolutionary theory informed by the spate of new data from modern genetics, molecular biology, paleobiology—from the new wave of the biologic revolution which spread after Darwin's announcement like a tsunami. The data are not all in. Crucial first appearances of major invertebrate groups are missing from the fossil record—but these early forms, sometimes modified larvae, tended to be fragile either by virtue of their actual malleability or by virtue of their scarcity and rapid variation into "hardened," successful forms. Lack of proof in this direction doesn't worry scientists. What neo-Darwinism seriously lacks, however, is a description of the actual mechanism of mutation in the chromosomal nucleotides.

In the larger sense, neo-Darwinism also lacks, for many, sheer plausibility. The triplet splendors of random mutation, natural selection, and Mendelian inheritance are neither energies nor gods; the words merely describe a gibbering tumult of materials. Many things are unexplained, many discrepancies unaccounted for. Appending a very modified neo-Lamarckism to Darwinism would solve many problems—and create new ones. Neo-Lamarckism holds, without any proof, that certain useful acquired characteristics may be inherited. Read C. H. Waddington, *The Strategy of the Genes,* and Arthur Koestler, *The Ghost in the Machine.* The Lamarckism/Darwinism issue is not only complex, hinging perhaps on whether DNA can be copied from RNA, but also politically hot. The upshot of it all is that while a form of Lamarckism holds sway in Russia, neo-Darwinism is supreme in the West, and its basic assumptions, though variously modified, are not overthrown.

So much for scientists. The rest of us didn't hear Darwin as a signal to dive down into the wet nucleus of a cell and surface with handfuls of strange new objects. We were still worried about the book with the unfortunate word in the title: *The Descent of Man.* It was dismaying to imagine great-grandma and great-grandpa effecting a literal, nimble descent from some liana-covered tree to terra firma, scratching themselves, and demanding bananas.

Fundamentalist Christians, of course, still reject Darwinism because it conflicts with the creation account in Genesis. Fundamentalist Christians have a very bad press. Ill feeling surfaces when, from time to time in small towns, they object again to the public schools' teaching evolutionary theory. Tragically, these people feel they have to make a choice between the Bible and modern science. They live and work in the same world as we, and know the derision they face from people whose areas of ignorance are perhaps different, who dismantled their mangers when they moved to town and threw out the baby with the straw.

Even less appealing in their response to the new evolutionary picture were, and are, the social Darwinists. Social Darwinists seized Herbert Spencer's phrase, "the survival of the fittest," applied it to capitalism, and used it to sanction ruthless and corrupt business practices. A social Darwinist is unlikely to identify himself with the term; social Darwinism is, as the saying goes, not a religion but a way of life. A modern social Darwinist wrote the slogan "If you're so smart, why ain't you rich?" The notion still obtains, I believe, wherever people seek power: that the race is to the swift, that everybody is *in* the race, with varying and merited degrees of success or failure, and that reward is its own virtue.

Philosophy reacted to Darwin with unaccustomed good cheer. William Paley's fixed and harmonious universe was gone, and with it its meticulous watchmaker god. Nobody mourned. Instead philosophy shrugged and turned its attention from first and final causes to analysis of certain values here in time. "Faith in progress," the man-in-the-street philosophy, collapsed in two world wars. Philosophers were more guarded; pragmatically, they held a very refined "faith in process"—which, it would seem, could hardly lose. Christian thinkers, too, outside of Fundamentalism, examined with fresh eyes the world's burgeoning change. Some Protestants, taking their cue from Whitehead, posited a dynamic god who lives alongside the universe, himself charged and changed by the process of becoming. Catholic Pierre Teilhard de Chardin, a paleontologist, examined the evolution of species itself, and discovered in that flow a surge toward complexity and consciousness, a free ascent capped with man and propelled from within and attracted from without by god, the holy freedom and awareness that is creation's beginning and end. And so forth. Like flatworms, like languages, ideas evolve. And they evolve, as Arthur Koestler suggests, not from hardened final forms, but from the softest plasmic germs in a cell's heart, in the nub of a word's root, in the supple flux of an open mind.

Darwin gave us time. Before Darwin (and Huxley, Wallace, et al) there was in the nineteenth century what must have been a fairly nauseating period: people knew about fossils of extinct species, but did not yet know about organic evolution. They thought the fossils were litter from a series of past creations. At any rate, for many, this creation, the world as we know it, had begun in 4004 B.C., a date set by Irish Archbishop James Ussher in the seventeenth century. We were all crouched in a small room against the comforting back wall, awaiting the millennium which had been gathering impetus since Adam and Eve. Up there was a universe, and down here would be a small strip of man come and gone, created, taught, redeemed, and gathered up in a bright twinkling, like a sprinkling of confetti torn from colored papers, tossed from windows, and swept from the streets by morning.

The Darwinian revolution knocked out the back wall, revealing eerie lighted landscapes as far back as we can see. Almost at once, Albert Einstein and astronomers with reflector telescopes and radio telescopes knocked out the other walls and the ceiling, leaving us sunlit, exposed, and drifting—leaving us puckers, albeit evolving puckers, on the inbound curve of space-time.

III

It all began in the Galápagos, with these finches. The finches in the Galápagos are called Darwin's finches; they are everywhere in the islands, sparrowlike, and almost identical but for their differing beaks. At first Darwin scarcely noticed their importance. But by 1839, when he revised his *Journal* of the *Beagle* voyage, he added a key sentence about the finches' beaks: "Seeing this gradation and diversity of structure in one small, intimately related group of birds, one might really fancy that from an original paucity of birds in this archipelago, one species had been taken and modified for different ends." And so it was.

The finches come when called. I don't know why it works, but it does. Scientists in the Galápagos have passed down the call: you say psssssh psssssh psssssh psssssh psssssh until you run out of breath; then you say it again until the island runs out of birds. You stand on a flat of sand by a shallow lagoon rimmed in mangrove thickets and call the birds right out of the sky. It works anywhere, from island to island.

Once, on the island of James, I was standing propped against a leafless *palo santo* tree on a semiarid inland slope, when the naturalist called the birds.

From other leafless *palo santo* trees flew the yellow warblers, speckling the air with bright bounced sun. Gray mockingbirds came running. And from the green prickly pear cactus, from the thorny acacias, sere grasses, bracken and manzanilla, from the loose black lava, the bare dust, the fern-hung mouths of caverns or the tops of sunlit logs—came the finches. They fell in from every direction like colored bits in a turning kaleidoscope. They circled and homed to a vortex, like a whirlwind of chips, like draining water. The tree on which I leaned was the vortex. A dry series of puffs hit my cheeks. Then a rough pulse from the tree's thin trunk met my palm and rang up my arm—and another, and another. The tree trunk agitated against my hand like a captured cricket: I looked up. The lighting birds were rocking the tree. It was an appearing act: before there were barren branches; now there were birds like leaves.

Darwin's finches are not brightly colored; they are black, gray, brown, or faintly olive. Their names are even duller: the large ground finch, the medium ground finch, the small ground finch; the large insectivorous tree finch; the vegetarian tree finch; the cactus ground finch, and so forth. But the beaks are interesting, and the beaks' origins even more so.

Some finches wield chunky parrot beaks modified for cracking seeds. Some have slender warbler beaks, short for nabbing insects, long for probing plants. One sports the long chisel beak of a woodpecker; it bores wood for insect grubs and often uses a twig or cactus spine as a pickle fork when the grub won't dislodge. They have all evolved, fanwise, from one bird.

The finches evolved in isolation. So did everything else on earth. With the finches, you can see how it happened. The Galápagos islands are near enough to the mainland that some strays could hazard there; they are far enough away that those strays could evolve in isolation from parent species. And the separate islands are near enough to each other for further dispersal, further isolation, and the eventual reassembling of distinct species. (In other words, finches blew to the Galápagos, blew to various islands, evolved into differing species, and blew back together again.) The tree finches and the ground finches, the woodpecker finch and the warbler finch, veered into being on isolated rocks. The witless green sea shaped those beaks as surely as it shaped the beaches. Now on the finches in the *palo santo* tree you see adaptive radiation's results, a fluorescent splay of horn. It is as though an archipelago were an arpeggio, a rapid series of distinct but related notes. If the Galápagos had been one unified island, there would be one dull note, one super-dull finch.

IV

Now let me carry matters to an imaginary, and impossible, extreme. If the earth were one unified island, a smooth ball, we would all be one species, a tremulous muck. The fact is that when you get down to this business of species formation, you eventually hit some form of reproductive isolation. Cells tend to fuse. Cells tend to engulf each other; primitive creatures tend to move in on each other and on us, to colonize, aggregate, blur. (Within species, individuals have evolved immune reactions, which help preserve individual integrity; you might reject my liver—or someday my brain.) As much of the world's energy seems to be devoted to keeping us apart as was directed to bringing us here in the first place. All sorts of different creatures can mate and produce fertile offspring: two species of snapdragon, for instance, or mallard and pintail ducks. But they don't. They live apart, so they don't mate. When you scratch the varying behaviors and conditions behind reproductive isolation, you find, ultimately, geographical isolation. Once the isolation has occurred, of course, forms harden out, enforcing reproductive isolation, so that snapdragons will never mate with pintail ducks.

Geography is the key, the crucial accident of birth. A piece of protein could be a snail, a sea lion, or a systems analyst, but it had to start somewhere. This is not science;

it is merely metaphor. And the landscape in which the protein "starts" shapes its end as surely as bowls shape water.

We have all, as it were, blown back together like the finches, and it's hard to imagine the isolation from parent species in which we evolved. The frail beginnings of great phyla are lost in the crushed histories of cells. Now we see the embellishments of random chromosomal mutations selected by natural selection and preserved in geographically isolate gene pools as *faits accomplis*, as the differentiated fringe of brittle knobs that is life as we know it. The process is still going on, but there is no turning back; it happened, in the cells. Geographical determination is not the cow-caught-in-a-crevice business I make it seem. I'm dealing in imagery, working toward a picture.

Geography is life's limiting factor. Speciation—life itself—is ultimately a matter of warm and cool currents, rich and bare soils, deserts and forests, fresh and salt waters, deltas and jungles and plains. Species arise in isolation. A plaster cast is as intricate as its mold; life is a gloss on geography. And if you dig your fists into the earth and crumble geography, you strike geology. Climate is the wind of the mineral earth's rondure, tilt, and orbit modified by local geological conditions. The Pacific Ocean, the Negev Desert, and the rain forest in Brazil are local geological conditions. So are the slow carp pools and splashing trout riffles of any backyard creek. It is all, God help us, a matter of rocks.

The rocks shape life like hands around swelling dough. In Virginia, the salamanders vary from mountain ridge to mountain ridge; so do the fiddle tunes the old men play. All this is because it is hard to move from mountain to mountain. These are not merely anomalous details. This is what life is all about: salamanders, fiddle tunes, you and me and things, the split and burr of it all, the fizz into particulars. No mountains and one salamander, one fiddle tune, would be a lesser world. No continents, no fiddlers. No possum, no sop, no taters. The earth, without form, is void.

The mountains are time's machines; in effect, they roll out protoplasm like printers' rollers pressing out news. But life is already part of the landscape, a limiting factor in space; life too shapes life. Geology's rocks and climate have already become Brazil's rain forest, yielding shocking bright birds. To say that all life is an interconnected membrane, a weft of linkages like chain mail, is truism. But in this case, too, the Galápagos islands afford a clear picture.

On Santa Cruz island, for instance, the saddleback carapaces of tortoises enable them to stretch high and reach the succulent pads of prickly pear cactus. But the prickly pear cactus on that island, and on other tortoise islands, has evolved a treelike habit; those lower pads get harder to come by. Without limiting factors, the two populations could stretch right into the stratosphere.

_Ça va._ It goes on everywhere, tit for tat, action and reaction, triggers and inhibitors ascending in a spiral like spatting butterflies. Within life, we are pushing each other around. How many animal forms have evolved just so because there are, for instance, trees? We pass the

nitrogen around, and vital gases; we feed and nest, pluck-
ing this and that and planting seeds. The protoplasm
responds, nudged and nudging, bearing the news.

And the rocks themselves shall be moved. The rocks
themselves are not pure necessity, given, like vast, complex molds around which the rest of us swirl. They heave
to their own necessities, to stirrings and prickings from
within and without.

The mountains are no more fixed than the stars. Granite, for example, contains much oxygen and is relatively
light. It "floats." When granite forms under the earth's
crust, great chunks of it bob up, I read somewhere, like
dumplings. The continents themselves are beautiful pea-
green boats. The Galápagos archipelago as a whole is
surfing toward Ecuador; South America is sliding toward
the Galápagos; North America, too, is sailing westward.
We're on floating islands, shaky ground.

So the rocks shape life, and then life shapes life, and
the rocks are moving. The completed picture needs one
more element: life shapes the rocks.

Life is more than a live green scum on a dead pool, a
shimmering scurf like slime mold on rock. Look at the
planet. Everywhere freedom twines its way around necessity, inventing new strings of occasions, lassoing time
and putting it through its varied and spirited paces. Everywhere live things lash at the rocks. Softness is vulnerable, but it has a will; tube worms bore and coral atolls
rise. Lichens in delicate lobes are chewing the granite
mountains; forests in serried ranks trammel the hills. Man
has more freedom than other live things; anti-entropi-

cally, he batters a bigger dent in the given, damming the rivers, planting the plains, drawing in his mind's eye dotted lines between the stars.

The old ark's a moverin'. Each live thing wags its home waters, rumples the turf, rearranges the air. The rocks press out protoplasm; the protoplasm pummels the rocks. It could be that this is the one world, and that world a bright snarl.

Like boys on dolphins, the continents ride their crustal plates. New lands shoulder up from the waves, and old lands buckle under. The very landscapes heave; change burgeons into change. Gray granite bobs up, red clay compresses; yellow sandstone tilts, surging in forests, incised by streams. The mountains tremble, the ice rasps back and forth, and the protoplasm furls in shock waves, up the rock valleys and down, ramifying possibilities, riddling the mountains. Life and the rocks, like spirit and matter, are a fringed matrix, lapped and lapping, clasping and held. It is like hand washing hand. It is like hand washing hand and the whole tumult hurled. The planet spins, rapt inside its intricate mists. The galaxy is a flung thing, loose in the night, and our solar system is one of many dotted campfires ringed with tossed rocks. What shall we sing?

What shall we sing, while the fire burns down? We can sing only specifics, time's rambling tune, the places we have seen, the faces we have known. I will sing you the Galápagos islands, the sea lions soft on the rocks. It's all still happening there, in real light, the cool currents

upwelling, the finches falling on the wind, the shearwaters looping the waves. I could go back, or I could go
on; or I could sit down, like Kubla Khan:

> Weave a circle round him thrice,
>   And close your eyes with holy dread,
> For he on honey-dew hath fed,
>   And drunk the milk of Paradise.

A Field of Silence

THERE IS A PLACE called "the farm" where I lived once, in a time that was very lonely. Fortunately I was unconscious of my loneliness then, and felt it only deeply, bewildered, in the half-bright way that a puppy feels pain.

I loved the place, and still do. It was an ordinary farm, a calf-raising, haymaking farm, and very beautiful. Its flat, messy pastures ran along one side of the central portion of a quarter-mile road in the central part of an island, an island in Puget Sound, on the Washington coast, so that from the high end of the road you could look west toward the Pacific, to the sound and its hundred islands, and from the other end—and from the farm— you could see east to the water between you and the mainland, and beyond it the mainland's mountains slicked with snow.

I liked the clutter about the place, the way everything blossomed or seeded or rusted; I liked the hundred half-finished projects, the smells, and the way the animals always broke loose. It is calming to herd animals. Often a regular rodeo breaks out—two people and a clever cow can kill a morning—but still, it is calming. You laugh for a while, exhausted, and silence is restored; the beasts are back in their pastures, the fences are not fixed but disguised as if they were fixed, ensuring the animals' temporary resignation; and a great calm descends, a lack of urgency, a sense of having to invent something to do until the next time you must run and chase cattle.

The farm seemed eternal in the crude way the earth does—extending, that is, a very long time. The farm was as old as earth, always there, as old as the island, the Platonic form of "farm," of human society itself, a piece of land eaten and replenished a billion summers, a piece of land worked on, lived on, grown over, plowed under, and stitched again and again, with fingers or with leaves, in and out and into human life's thin weave. I lived there once.

I lived there once and I have seen, from behind the barn, the long roadside pastures heaped with silence. Behind the rooster, suddenly, I saw the silence heaped on the fields like trays. That day the green hayfields supported silence evenly sown; the fields bent just so under the even pressure of silence, bearing it, palming it aloft: cleared fields, part of a land, a planet, that did not buckle beneath the heel of silence, nor split up scattered to bits, but instead lay secret, disguised as time and matter as though that were nothing, ordinary—disguised as fields like those which bear the silence only because they are spread, and the silence spreads over them, great in size.

I do not want, I think, ever to see such a sight again. That there is loneliness here I had granted, in the abstract—but not, I thought, inside the light of God's presence, inside his sanction, and signed by his name.

I lived alone in the farmhouse and rented; the owners, in their twenties, lived in another building just over the yard. I had been reading and restless for two or three days. It was morning. I had just read at breakfast an Updike story, "Packed Dirt, Churchgoing, A Dying Cat, A Traded Car," which moved me. I heard our own farmyard rooster and two or three roosters across the street screeching. I quit the house, hoping at heart to see either of the owners, but immediately to watch our rooster as he crowed.

It was Saturday morning late in the summer, in early September, clear-aired and still. I climbed the barnyard fence between the poultry and the pastures; I watched the red rooster, and the rooster, reptilian, kept one alert and alien eye on me. He pulled his extravagant neck to its maximum length, hauled himself high on his legs, stretched his beak as if he were gagging, screamed, and blinked. It was a ruckus. The din came from everywhere, and only the most rigorous application of reason could persuade me that it proceeded in its entirety from this lone and maniac bird.

After a pause, the roosters across the street started, answering the proclamation, or cranking out another round, arhythmically, interrupting. In the same way there is no pattern nor sense to the massed stridulations of cicadas; their skipped beats, enjambments, and failed alterations jangle your spirits, as though each of those thousand insects, each with identical feelings, were stubbornly deaf to the others, and loudly alone.

I shifted along the fence to see if either of the owners was coming or going. To the rooster I said nothing, but only stared. And he stared at me; we were both careful to keep the wooden fence slat from our line of sight, so that his profiled eye and my two eyes could meet. From time to time I looked beyond the pastures to learn if anyone might be seen on the road.

When I was turned away in this manner, the silence gathered and struck me. It bashed me broadside from the heavens above me like yard goods; ten acres of fallen, invisible sky choked the fields. The pastures on either side of the road turned green in a surrealistic fashion, monstrous, impeccable, as if they were holding their breaths. The roosters stopped. All the things of the world—the fields and the fencing, the road, a parked orange truck—were stricken and self-conscious. A world pressed down on their surfaces, a world battered just within their surfaces, and that real world, so near to emerging, had got stuck.

There was only silence. It was the silence of matter caught in the act and embarrassed. There were no cells moving, and yet there were cells. I could see the shape of the land, how it lay holding silence. Its poise and its stillness were unendurable, like the ring of the silence you hear in your skull when you're little and notice you're living, the ring which resumes later in life when you're sick.

There were flies buzzing over the dirt by the henhouse, moving in circles and buzzing, black dreams in chips off the one long dream, the dream of the regular world. But the silent fields were the real world, eternity's outpost in time, whose look I remembered but never like this, this God-blasted, paralyzed day. I felt myself tall and vertical, in a blue shirt, self-conscious, and wishing to die. I heard the flies again; I looked at the rooster who was frozen looking at me.

Then at last I heard whistling, human whistling far on the air, and I was not able to bear it. I looked around, heartbroken; only at the big yellow Charolais farm far up the road was there motion—a woman, I think, dressed in pink, and pushing a wheelbarrow easily over the grass. It must have been she who was whistling and heaping on top of the silence those hollow notes of song. But the slow sound of the music—the beautiful sound of the music ringing the air like a stone bell—was isolate and detached. The notes spread into the general air and became the weightier part of silence, silence's last straw. The distant woman and her wheelbarrow were flat and detached, like mechanized and pink-painted properties for a stage. I stood in pieces, afraid I was unable to move. Something had unhinged the world. The houses and roadsides and pastures were buckling under the silence. Then a Labrador, black, loped up the distant driveway, fluid and cartoonlike, toward the pink woman. I had to try to turn away. Holiness is a force, and like the others can be resisted. It was given, but I didn't want to see it, God or no God. It was as if God had said, "I am here, but not as you have known me. This is the look of silence, and of loneliness unendurable; it too has always been mine, and now will be yours." I was not ready for a life of sorrow, sorrow deriving from knowledge I could just as well stop at the gate.

I turned away, willful, and the whole show vanished. The realness of things disassembled. The whistling became ordinary, familiar; the air above the fields released its pressure and the fields lay hooded as before. I myself could act. Looking to the rooster I whistled to him myself, softly, and some hens appeared at the chicken house window, greeted the day, and fluttered down.

Several months later, walking past the farm on the way to a volleyball game, I remarked to a friend, by way of information, "There are angels in those fields." Angels! That silence so grave and so stricken, that choked and unbearable green! I have rarely been so surprised at something I've said. Angels! What are angels? I had never thought of angels, in any way at all.

From that time I began to think of angels. I considered that sights such as I had seen of the silence must have been shared by the people who said they saw angels. I began to review the thing I had seen that morning. My impression now of those fields is of thousands of spirits— spirits trapped, perhaps, by my refusal to call them more fully, or by the paralysis of my own spirit at that time— thousands of spirits, angels in fact, almost discernible to the eye, and whirling. If pressed I would say they were three or four feet from the ground. Only their motion was clear (clockwise, if you insist); that, and their beauty unspeakable.

There are angels in those fields, and, I presume, in all fields, and everywhere else. I would go to the lions for this conviction, to witness this fact. What all this means about perception, or language, or angels, or my own sanity, I have no idea.

God in the Doorway

ONE COLD CHRISTMAS EVE I was up unnaturally late because we had all gone out to dinner—my parents, my baby sister, and I. We had come home to a warm living room, and Christmas Eve. Our stockings drooped from the mantel; beside them, a special table bore a bottle of ginger ale and a plate of cookies.

I had taken off my fancy winter coat and was standing on the heat register to bake my shoe soles and warm my bare legs. There was a commotion at the front door; it opened, and cold wind blew around my dress.

Everyone was calling me. "Look who's here! Look who's here!" I looked. It was Santa Claus. Whom I never—ever—wanted to meet. Santa Claus was looming in the doorway and looking around for me. My mother's voice was thrilled: "Look who's here!" I ran upstairs.

Like everyone in his right mind, I feared Santa Claus, thinking he was God. I was still thoughtless and brute, reactive. I knew right from wrong, but had barely tested the possibility of shaping my own behavior, and then only from fear, and not yet from love. Santa Claus was an old man whom you never saw, but who nevertheless saw you; he knew when you'd been bad or good. He knew when you'd been bad or good! And I had been bad.

My mother called and called, enthusiastic, pleading; I wouldn't come down. My father encouraged me; my sister howled. I wouldn't come down, but I could bend over the stairwell and see: Santa Claus stood in the doorway with night over his shoulder, letting in all the cold air of the sky; Santa Claus stood in the doorway monstrous and bright, powerless, ringing a loud bell and repeating Merry Christmas, Merry Christmas. I never came down. I don't know who ate the cookies.

For so many years now I have known that this Santa Claus was actually a rigged-up Miss White, who lived across the street, that I confuse the *dramatis personae* in my mind, making of Santa Claus, God, and Miss White an awesome, vulnerable trinity. This is really a story about Miss White.

Miss White was old; she lived alone in the big house across the street. She liked having me around; she plied me with cookies, taught me things about the world, and tried to interest me in finger painting, in which she herself took great pleasure. She would set up easels in her kitchen, tack enormous slick soaking papers to their frames, and paint undulating undersea scenes: horizontal smears of color sparked by occasional vertical streaks which were understood to be fixed kelp. I liked her. She meant no harm on earth, and yet half a year after her failed visit as Santa Claus, I ran from her again.

That day, a day of the following summer, Miss White and I knelt in her yard while she showed me a magnifying glass. It was a large, strong hand lens. She lifted my hand and, holding it very still, focused a dab of sunshine on my palm. The glowing crescent wobbled, spread, and finally contracted to a point. It burned; I was burned; I ripped my hand away and ran home crying. Miss White called after me, sorry, explaining, but I didn't look back.

Even now I wonder: if I meet God, will he take and hold my bare hand in his, and focus his eye on my palm, and kindle that spot and let me burn?

But no. It is I who misunderstood everything and let everybody down. Miss White, God, I am sorry I ran from you. I am still running, running from that knowledge, that eye, that love from which there is no refuge. For you meant only love, and love, and I felt only fear, and pain. So once in Israel love came to us incarnate, stood in the doorway between two worlds, and we were all afraid.

Mirages

ALL SUMMER LONG MIRAGES APPEAR OVER PUGET SOUND, mirages appear and vanish. While they last they mince and maul the islands and waters, and put us in thrall to our senses.

It is as though summer itself were a mirage, a passive dream of pleasure, itself untrue. For in winter the beaches lie empty; the gulls languish; the air is a reasonable stuff, chilled and lidded by clouds. We light the lamps early; we fasten the doors. We live in the mind. The water everywhere is vacant; the tankers alone still pass, their low diesel vibrations and their powerful wakes adding to the wind's whine and waves only a moment's more commotion; then they are gone.

No one is about. Although our island cabin is right

on the beach, so we can see many miles of shoreline, in winter we see only a single human light. At dusk, someone in Canada lights a lamp; it burns near the shore of Saturna, a Canadian island across Haro Strait, seven nautical miles away. We look at this lone light all winter, wondering if the people there are as cheered by our light as we are by theirs. We plan to visit them in the summer and introduce ourselves, but we never do. In winter there is nobody, nothing. If you see a human figure, or a boat on the water, you grab binoculars.

But in summer everything fills. The day itself widens and stretches almost around the clock; these are very high latitudes, higher than Labrador's. You want to run all night. Summer people move into the houses that had stood empty, unseen, and unnoticed all winter. The gulls scream all day and smash cockles; by August they are bringing the kids. Volleyball games resume on the sand flat; someone fires up the sauna; in the long dusk, at eleven o'clock, half a dozen beach fires people the shore. The bay fills up with moored boats and the waters beyond fill with pleasure craft, hundreds of cruisers and sailboats and speedboats. The wind dies and stays dead, and these fierce waters, which in winter feel the strongest windstorms in the country, become suddenly like a resort lake, some tamed dammed reservoir, the plaything of any manjack with a motor and a hull. Surely this is mirage. The heat is on, and the light is on, and someone is pouring drinks. On the beach we dip freshly dug clams in hot butter; we eat raw oysters from their shells. We play catch or sail a dinghy or holler; we have sand in our hair, calluses on our feet, hot brown skin on our arms. This is the life of the senses, the life of pleasures. It is mirage on the half shell. It vanishes like any fun, and the empty winds resume.

So much for the moral. The story is even simpler, a matter of gross physics and the senses. It is just that mirages abound here.

When winter's cloud cover vanishes, the naked planet lies exposed to marvels. The heated summer air, ground under cold northern air, becomes lenticular, shaped like a lentil or a lens. When the very air is a lens, how the mind ignites! We live among high heaps of mirages, among pickets and pilings and stacks of waving light. We live in a hall of mirrors rimmed by a horizon holey and warped.

Even now as I write, a mirage is pulling Saturna island like taffy. The island's far shores are starting to yawn and heave from the water. What had been a flat beach has become a high cliff. I wonder: are the people still there, the people whose lamp we could see in the winter? Have they been stretched too, and pulled out of shape? If we went to meet them now, would we find them teetering in their garden like giraffes, unable to reach the ground and tend to their peas?

Few others see the mirages. I certainly never saw them until an article in *Scientific American* alerted me. Mirages, like anything unusual, are hard to see. The mind expects the usual. If a tanker appears to be plying ten yards above the surface of the water, the mind will pour in enough water to float the tanker properly, and deceive the eyes, and hush them with their Chicken-Little message for the brain. Brain never knows. "What mirages?" everyone says.

There are two other unexpected things about mirages, both of which, incidentally, are true of rainbows as well. One is that they photograph very well; the *Scientific American* article included a print which showed people walking about in the middle of a sailing fleet. The other is that enlarging lenses—telescopes, telephoto lenses, binoculars—far from betraying the shabbiness of the illusions, instead confirm and clarify them. I always look at mirages through binoculars; the binoculars' magnification adds both detail and substance to the vision. Great shimmering patches of color appear over the water, expanding and contracting in slats like venetian blinds; the binoculars enlarge the sight. The elongate cliffs of Saturna Island, rearing enormously from where no cliffs have ever been— these high palisades have a certain translucent, faked look to the naked eye, as if their matter, being so pulled, had stretched thin; but through binoculars they are as opaque as other cliffs, cliffy, solid, true headlands, and doubly mysterious.

Yesterday I stood on the beach and watched two light shows at once. It was fair and calm and hot; I faced a string of islands to the west. To the south I saw, spanning a wide channel between islands, a long crescendo-shaped warp, into which innocent little sailboats would wander and be wholly transformed into things glorious. A twenty-foot sloop entered the narrow end of the mirage. Before my eyes the sloop began to expand. Its mast grew like a beanstalk; its sails rose up like waterspouts. Soon the reckless boat, running down the light air and down the warp's widening crescendo, was flying a 150-foot spinnaker! There was a fleet of such boats in the sound. They were gigantic, top-heavy dream-sailers, mythic big ships sailing solar wind and stringing their dwarfed hulls after them like sea anchors. Now there, into the crescendo, went a white cabin cruiser, sport fishing for salmon; and here, at the other end, emerged a wedding cake, a wedding cake leaving a wake and steered by God knows what elongate gibbon of a vacationer at the wheel.

While these boats to the south were blooming transfigured over calm water, to the north the water itself was apparently erupting and bending into hills and valleys. The water itself, I say, had grown absurd, sloping this way and that in long parallel ridges like those of a washboard. There were no waves; instead the smooth water itself lay seemingly jagged and rucked as Appalachians, as enormous stairways, pleated into long lines of sixty-foot ridges and valleys. In this mess of slopes a host of white cabin cruisers was struggling uphill and down. The boats crawled up and over the pitches like tanks over earthworks and trenches; or their bows aimed at heaven, their hulls churning directly up ridges so steep I thought they would all flip over backward like so many unicycles. It was flat calm. Only that one patch of water was berserk, as if it had wearied of the monotony of being a seascape year after year and was now seeking coarsely to emulate the ranged bumps of land.

Then the show pulled out. In the south the giant sails and the wedding cake cruisers emerged from the dazzle suddenly ordinary in proportion and humble. Nevertheless, from their masts and over their cabins hung some remembered radiance, some light-shot tatters of their recent glory. They continued across the horizon as creatures who had been touched, like the straggling and shining caravans of the wilderness generation as it quit Sinai. In the north the little cruisers I had watched now steered from the canyons and found regular waters, which looked mighty dull. Other boats still hazarded into the ridges, but the heights were no longer so fearsome; gradually, over the space of an hour, the mountains sank back to the water, and the water closed over them in the way that water has always closed over everything, in literature and in fact: as if they had never been.

Sojourner

IF SURVIVAL IS AN ART, then mangroves are artists of the beautiful: not only that they exist at all—smooth-barked, glossy-leaved, thickets of lapped mystery—but that they can and do exist as floating islands, as trees upright and loose, alive and homeless on the water.

I have seen mangroves, always on tropical ocean shores, in Florida and in the Galápagos. There is the red mangrove, the yellow, the button, and the black. They are all short, messy trees, waxy-leaved, laced all over with aerial roots, woody arching buttresses, and weird leathery berry pods. All this tangles from a black muck soil, a black muck matted like a mud-sopped rag, a muck without any other plants, shaded, cold to the touch, tracked at the water's edge by herons and nosed by sharks.

It is these shoreline trees which, by a fairly common accident, can become floating islands. A hurricane flood or a riptide can wrest a tree from the shore, or from the mouth of a tidal river, and hurl it into the ocean. It floats. It is a mangrove island, blown.

There are floating islands on the planet; it amazes me. Credulous Pliny described some islands thought to be mangrove islands floating on a river. The people called these river islands *the dancers*, "because in any consort of musicians singing, they stir and move at the stroke of the feet, keeping time and measure."

Trees floating on rivers are less amazing than trees floating on the poisonous sea. A tree cannot live in salt. Mangrove trees exude salt from their leaves; you can see it, even on shoreline black mangroves, as a thin white crust. Lick a leaf and your tongue curls and coils; your mouth's a heap of salt.

Nor can a tree live without soil. A hurricane-born mangrove island may bring its own soil to the sea. But other mangrove trees make their own soil—and their own islands—from scratch. These are the ones which interest me. The seeds germinate in the fruit on the tree. The germinated embryo can drop anywhere—say, onto a dab of floating muck. The heavy root end sinks; a leafy plumule unfurls. The tiny seedling, afloat, is on its way. Soon aerial roots shooting out in all directions trap debris. The sapling's networks twine, the interstices narrow, and water calms in the lee. Bacteria thrive on organic broth; amphipods swarm. These creatures grow and die at the trees' wet feet. The soil thickens, accumulating rainwater, leaf rot, seashells, and guano; the island spreads.

More seeds and more muck yield more trees on the

new island. A society grows, interlocked in a tangle of dependencies. The island rocks less in the swells. Fish throng to the backwaters stilled in snarled roots. Soon, Asian mudskippers—little four-inch fish—clamber up the mangrove roots into the air and peer about from periscope eyes on stalks, like snails. Oysters clamp to submersed roots, as do starfish, dog whelk, and the creatures that live among tangled kelp. Shrimp seek shelter there, limpets a holdfast, pelagic birds a rest.

And the mangrove island wanders on, afloat and adrift. It walks teetering and wanton before the wind. Its fate and direction are random. It may bob across an ocean and catch on another mainland's shores. It may starve or dry while it is still a sapling. It may topple in a storm, or pitchpole. By the rarest of chances, it may stave into another mangrove island in a crash of clacking roots, and mesh. What it is most likely to do is drift anywhere in the alien ocean, feeding on death and growing, netting a makeshift soil as it goes, shrimp in its toes and terns in its hair.

We could do worse.

I alternate between thinking of the planet as home—dear and familiar stone hearth and garden—and as a hard land of exile in which we are all sojourners. Today I favor the latter view. The word "sojourner" occurs often in the English Old Testament. It invokes a nomadic people's sense of vagrancy, a praying people's knowledge of estrangement, a thinking people's intuition of sharp loss: "For we are strangers before thee, and sojourners, as were all our fathers: our days on the earth are as a shadow, and there is none abiding."

We don't know where we belong, but in times of sorrow it doesn't seem to be here, here with these silly pansies and witless mountains, here with sponges and hardeyed birds. In times of sorrow the innocence of the other creatures—from whom and with whom we evolved—seems a mockery. Their ways are not our ways. We seem set among them as among lifelike props for a tragedy—or a broad lampoon—on a thrust rock stage.

It doesn't seem to be here that we belong, here where space is curved, the earth is round, we're all going to die, and it seems as wise to stay in bed as budge. It is strange here, not quite warm enough, or too warm, too leafy, or inedible, or windy, or dead. It is not, frankly, the sort of home for people one would have thought of—although I lack the fancy to imagine another.

The planet itself is a sojourner in airless space, a wet ball flung across nowhere. The few objects in the universe scatter. The coherence of matter dwindles and crumbles toward stillness. I have read, and repeated, that our solar system as a whole is careering through space toward a point east of Hercules. Now I wonder: what could that possibly mean, east of Hercules? Isn't space curved? When we get "there," how will our course change, and why? Will we slide down the universe's inside arc like mud slung at a wall? Or what sort of welcoming shore is this east of Hercules? Surely we don't anchor there, and disembark, and sweep into dinner with our host. Does someone cry, "Last stop, last stop"? At any rate, east of Hercules, like east of Eden, isn't a place to call home. It is a course without direction; it is "out." And we are cast.

These are enervating thoughts, the thoughts of despair. They crowd back, unbidden, when human life as it unrolls goes ill, when we lose control of our lives or the illusion of control, and it seems that we are not moving toward any end but merely blown. Our life seems cursed to be a wiggle merely, and a wandering without end. Even nature is hostile and poisonous, as though it were impossible for our vulnerability to survive on these acrid stones.

Whether these thoughts are true or not I find less interesting than the possibilities for beauty they may hold. We are down here in time, where beauty grows. Even if things are as bad as they could possibly be, and as meaningless, then matters of truth are themselves indifferent; we may as well please our sensibilities and, with as much spirit as we can muster, go out with a buck and wing.

The planet is less like an enclosed spaceship—spaceship earth—than it is like an exposed mangrove island beautiful and loose. We the people started small and have since accumulated a great and solacing muck of soil, of human culture. We are rooted in it; we are bearing it with us across nowhere. The word "nowhere" is our cue: the consort of musicians strikes up, and we in the chorus stir and move and start twirling our hats. A mangrove island turns drift to dance. It creates its own soil as it goes, rocking over the salt sea at random, rocking day and night and round the sun, rocking round the sun and out toward east of Hercules.

Aces and Eights

I

I AM HERE against my good judgment. I understood long ago just what it would be like; I knew that the weekend would be, above all, over. At home at my desk I doodled on tablets and imagined myself and the child standing side by side on the riverbank behind the cottage in the woods, standing on the riverbank and watching the blossoms float down, or the dead leaves float down, or just the water—whatever it would be—and thinking, each of us: remember this, remember this now, this weekend in the country. And I knew that instead of seeing (let alone remembering) the blossoms, or the leaves, or whatever, the child and I would each see and remember some dim picture of our own selves as figures side by side on the riverbank, as figures in our own future memories, as focal points for some absurd, manufactured nostalgia.

There was no use going. At best, we would miss the whole thing. If any part of the weekend should prove in the least pleasant, and worth trying to remember on that account, or on account of its never-to-be-repeated quality, it would be unbearable. Who would subject a child to such suffering? On the other hand, maybe it would rain.

I decided, in short, not to go. The child is nine, and already morbidly nostalgic and given to wringing meaningful moments out of our least occasions. I am thirty-five; my tolerance for poignancy has diminished to the vanishing point. If I wish, and I do not, I can have never-to-be-repeated moments, however dreadful, anywhere and anytime, simply by calling that category to mind.

But we are here: the child, and I, and the dog. It is a weekend in mid-July. We will leave here Sunday morning early.

The cottage is in the Appalachians, in a long-settled river valley. The forest is in its ninth or twelfth growth: oak-maple-hickory, with hemlock and laurel in the mountain gorges. It is the same everywhere in the Appalachians, from Maine to Georgia. There is no place else in the fifty states where you could build a 2,050-mile linear trail through country that changes so little.

The ridges are dry—blackjack oak, berry bushes, and pine—and steep. Near here there is a place on a steep mountain called Carson's Castle. One summer many years ago a neighbor, Noah Very, took me and my cousins on an outing to this Carson's Castle. It is nothing but a cave in the mountaintop with a stone ledge in front of it. The ledge overhangs the next valley so far that you have to look behind you, between your feet, to see the stream far below. In the eighteenth century, this stream became part of the state line.

Mr. Very walked us children up there and told us that when the Indians chased Mr. Carson—some time ago— he ran up the mountain and hid in the cave. And when the Indians, who were naturally conducting their chase Indian file, attained the cliff edge, each paused to wonder where Mr. Carson might have gone. Mr. Carson took advantage of their momentary confusion by pushing them, one by one, from the ledge—from the ledge, from the mountain, and as it would happen, out of state. He pushed them until there were none. That, at any rate, is the legend. An old Indian legend, I believe.

Literalist and begrudger as I was and am, I expected to see a rather fancy castle on the mountaintop that day, and was disappointed. But now I choose to remember this outing as a raging success, and am grateful to "Count" Noah Very, and intend to bake him a cake while we are here, although he has long since turned into an old, disagreeable coot.

The ridges are dry, I say, and the bottomlands are wet. There are sycamores on the riverbanks, and tulip poplars, willows, and silver maples; there is jewelweed in the sun and rhododendron in the shade. The cottage is in a small clearing in the woods on a riverbank.

The child has discovered the blackboard in the children's room. She wheels it into the living room where I sit and writes on it, "I love Francis Burn." She says that Francis Burn is a boy in her school, going into the sixth grade. When I ask her what it is about Francis Burn that she loves, she answers that he is cute.

Once I knew a woman, who has since died, whose field was German philosophy. When I knew her she had just been widowed. Her husband—an old man, remote and stern—had held a university chair in intellectual history; between them they had written a dozen books. Once, when the woman and I were alone, she broke down. She broke down in grief, and cried in my arms, and repeated into my shoulder, "He was so cute!"

The child wheels the blackboard against a bare wall, to serve as our mural or graffito for the weekend. She is nine, beloved, as open-faced as the sky and as self-contained. I have watched her grow. As recently as three or four years ago, she had a young child's perfectly shallow receptiveness; she fitted into the world of time, it fitted into her, as thoughtlessly as sky fits its edges, or a river its banks. But as she has grown, her smile has widened with a touch of fear and her glance has taken on depth. Now she is aware of some of the losses you incur by being here—the extortionary rent you have to pay as long as you stay. We have lived together so often, and parted so many times, that the very sight of each other means loss. The ever-taller embrace of our hellos is a tearful affair, aware as we are of our imminent parting; fortunately the same anticipation cancels our goodbyes, and we embrace cheerfully, like long-lost kin at a reunion.

I have not been here in years. I think of it, though, when I cannot sleep; I stand on the bank and watch the river move, and watch the water's speckled reflections jiggle on the overarching boughs of sycamore, and jiggle on the sycamore's trunk, and on the bottoms of its leaves. Across the river I see pasture veined by the thin paths of cows. The cowpaths wobble over the floodplain and cut around the junipers and clumps of thistle or rose; they climb a close-cropped slope whose every bump and ripple shows, a slope which is actually the foot of a wooded mountain. The pasture ends, and the forest begins, in a saggy wooden fence.

Personally, I find the keeping of golden Guernseys rather an affectation. But the actual cows themselves, I allow, are innocent. The actual cows themselves, in this soporific vision of mine, are splayed about the landscape, lending solid areas of warm color to a field otherwise pallidly, sentimentally, green. Behind their pasture is a border of woods, a sloping cornfield, and beyond, rolling ridges.

When we opened the cottage over an hour ago, I found a note taped to the icebox door. It read: "Matches in the tin box on mantel. Do not eat purple berries from bush by porch. Bulbs of creek grass OK, good boiled. Blue berries in woods make you sick." Accompanying the text were careful schematic drawings of the plants in question: pokeberry, something I do not recognize, huckleberry. Huckleberries are perfectly edible. Many people have used this cottage over the years—including, I suppose, grouches with sour stomachs, and hoaxers. If I were interested in such things, I would have to do all the research again. I am not interested in such things. It has been quite a while since I sampled bits of the landscape. I have brought a box of groceries from home.

It is all woods on this side of the river—woods, and a surprising number of paved roads. A steep driveway leads from a hill down to the cottage; you park beside the cottage on the grass, on that thin, round-bladed, bluish grass that grows under trees. The cottage rests on cinder blocks; a sort of yard slopes to the river's edge.

In the 1920s, American manufacturers started prefabricating summer cottages; this cottage is one of the first of those. It does not look prefabricated. It is just on the fussy side of idyllic—white frame, two bedrooms, a big screened porch, and lots of painted latticework. When you lie in bed you can see the big bolts in the ceiling that hold the house together. The bolts are painted white, like everything else.

You know what it is to open up a cottage. You barge in with your box of groceries and your duffelbag full of books. You drop them on a counter and rush to the far window to look out. I would say that coming into a cottage is like being born, except we do not come into the world with a box of groceries and a duffelbag full of books—unless you want to take these as metonymic symbols for culture. Opening up a summer cottage is like being born in this way: at the moment you enter, you have all the time you are ever going to have.

The child maintains—she has always maintained—that she remembers being born. It is a surefire attention-getter. "I remember," she says, "the light hurt my eyes." Many of her anecdotes are literary like this, and more than a little self-pitying. Should I stop hugging her so much?

Filling the window's frame, crowding each of its nine square panes, is the river, moving down.

The yellow afternoon light has faded from the water and the blue evening light is fading; the sycamore branches over the bank are flattening and growing dark. I see the sky on the running river. Blue, it shatters and pulls; blue, it catches and pools behind a rock. The sun is down behind the mountains, but not yet down behind the world.

The child and I go to play in the water. We leave the cottage, crouch on the bank, and send sticks down the river. Soon the night is too dark for us to see. We fetch some candle stubs from the house; we fetch some flat kindling from the woodpile; we light the candles, stick them to the flat wood, and launch them into the river. The river and the sky are just visible as blueness, bordered everywhere by indecipherable black. Now we can see the candle flames mark their own passage. We watch them wander above the water; we watch them wobble downstream and gutter out, one by one, just before they would have rounded the black, invisible bend.

"You cannot kill time," I read once, "without injuring eternity." Our setting the candles afloat down the river—

was this not a pretty thing to do? Why, when we were actually seeing the candles wobble down the river, did I think, this should be better? It seemed both to take too long and end too soon. As a memory, however, it is already looking good.

In bed I stare at the painted bolts in the walls. I hear the river outside the window, if I remember to listen. I read a magazine which contains instructions for jumping from a moving train:

> If for some extraordinary reason you have to jump off a moving train, look ahead and try to pick a spot that looks soft. Throw your pack and, as you jump, lean way back (this is the hard part) and take huge, leaping steps in the air. If you lean back far enough, and don't trip as you touch the ground, you will experience the rare thrill of running 35 to 40 miles an hour.

I cannot remember to listen for the river. Some elation keeps me from sleeping. I leave the bed and move to the porch, and stand in the open back door. There is a whippoorwill; there are stars over the pasture. It occurs to me to try to step down from the porch, which is moving in orbit at 68,400 miles an hour. I plan to take huge, leaping steps in the air. It will be, I realize, a rare thrill, but unfortunately I cannot find a landing space that looks soft.

II

Saturday morning, and all is changed. Sunlight on the table and on the shining wood floor is bright; the child and I walk around squinting and eager for action. How could I ever have wanted to read? I can scarcely credit that we played cards on this table last night, almost whispering, in a circle of lamplight not four feet across. Who, on a Saturday morning, would think of reading or playing cards? We are as changed from evening to morning, and as careless of yesterday, as if we had flown overnight to Nepal.

The child has found a bicycle under the porch; she wants to ride it. Incredibly, there is a bicycle pump half buried in the dry dirt beside it—a pump which works, once I scour and oil the shaft and screw dirt from the nozzle with a paperclip. I drag the bike out and stand it in the bluish grass at the foot of the driveway next to an apple tree. Pump the tires. I find a wrench to adjust the seat, find some WD-40 to loosen the bolt; lower the seat. Adjust the handlebars. Oil the chain and the steering column. Wash the seat, the handgrips, the fenders while I'm at it.

Throughout these tasks, which occupy the morning, the child and I are singing some old Dixieland standards: "The World Is Waiting for the Sunrise," "Cherokee," "Basin Street Blues"—most of which we have sung often before. When the bicycle is ready to roll, it is almost time for lunch. The child mounts the bike and wobbles up the driveway. She takes a right, turns down the hill, and vanishes, singing at the top of her lungs.

On the bluish grass under the apple tree are two wrenches, a can of WD-40, a hammer, a scouring pad, a straightened paperclip, a pile of dirty paper towels and sponges, a pail of dirty water, and the child's sweater. I am hungry. In all the history of the world, it has never been so late.

I do not know when the child will be back, or if she will want to take a walk. I haul out my notebooks and sit at the table.

The child bursts in, hale and enthusiastic. She has discovered a long loop route around which to ride. While she talks she reaches into the table's drawer and finds the deck of cards we brought. She sits at the table, rummages through the deck, and asks if we have any clothespins.

I am always amazed at how straight she sits in a chair, at how touching is the sight of her apparently boneless hands, and at how pleased she herself is with those hands, how conscious of them. She asked me once if she could insure them. Do we have any clothespins?

She wants clothespins to fasten some cards to her bicycle so that when the wheels turn the cards will slap in the spokes. She pulls from the deck a pair of aces and a pair of eights.

Last night we played poker, the two of us. We got popcorn butter on the cards; we used aspirin tablets as chips. In the course of the play I showed aces and eights—"dead man's hand"—so I told her about that. I told her we call aces and eights "dead man's hand" because Wild Bill Hickok was holding them in a poker game when he was shot in the back. I no longer remember precisely why someone shot Wild Bill Hickok in the back, but I made up something I hope she forgets before she passes it on.

I find her some spring clothespins in this pre-equipped cottage which apparently has everything needed for life on earth except poker chips. I make her a sandwich, and put it in a knapsack with a jar of milk, a banana, and a funny little riddle book I found last night. Off she goes.

Once, many years ago, there was a child of nine who loved Walter Milligan. One Saturday morning she was walking in the neighborhood of her school. She walked and thought, "The plain fact is—as I have heard so many times—that in several years' time I will not love Walter Milligan. I will very probably marry someone else. I will be untrue; I will forget Walter Milligan."

Deeply, unforgettably, she thought that if what they said about Walter Milligan was true, then the rest went with it: that she would one day like her sister, and that she would be glad she had taken piano lessons. She was standing at the curb, waiting for the light to change. It was all she could do to remember not to get run over, so she would live to betray herself. For a series of connected notions presented themselves: if all these passions of mine be overturned, then what will become of me? Then what am I now?

She seemed real enough to herself, willful and conscious, but she had to consider the possibility—the likelihood, even—that she was a short-lived phenomenon, a fierce, vanishing thing like a hard shower, or a transitional form like a tadpole or winter bud—not the thing in itself but a running start on the thing—and that she was being borne helplessly and against all her wishes to suicide, to the certain loss of self and all she held dear. Herself and all that she held dear—this particular combination of love for Walter Milligan, hatred of sister and piano lessons, etc.—would vanish, destroyed against her wishes by her own hand.

When she changed, where will that other person have gone? Could anyone keep her alive, this person here on the street, and her passions? Will the unthinkable adult that she would become remember her? Will she think she is stupid? Will she laugh at her?

She was a willful one, and she made a vow. The light changed; she crossed the street and set off up the sloping sidewalk by the school. I must be loyal, for no one else is. If this is the system, then I will buck it. I will until I die ride my bike and walk along these very streets, where I belong. I will until I die love Walter Milligan and hate my sister and read and walk in the woods. And I will never, not I, sit and drink and smoke and do nothing but talk.

Foremost in her vow was this, that she would remember the vow itself. She woke to her surroundings; it was cold. Even walking so fiercely uphill, she was cold, and illuminated by a powerful energy. To her left was the stone elementary school, deserted on Saturday. Across the street was a dark row of houses, stone and brick, with their pillared porches. The porch floors were painted red or gray or green. This was not her own neighborhood, but it was her turf. She pushed uphill to the next corner. She committed to memory the look of that block, that neighborhood: the familiar cracked sidewalk, how pale it was, how sand collected in its cracks; the sycamores; the muffled sky.

Now it is early Saturday afternoon—the center of the weekend.

I am sitting under the sycamore on the riverbank below the cottage, just below the driveway. The dog and I have returned from a walk through the woods by the river upstream. Now I sit and look around and try to comfort the dog, who, on his part, is trying to persuade me to continue our walk downstream to New Orleans.

It is the height of day in the height of summer—mid-July. This means that the sky essentially does not exist, or is not, at any rate, a thing you would care to examine. Under the sky in the distance ahead roll some hazy wooded ridges—the mountains. Below them are crowded slopes of field corn. In their floodplain pasture a dozen brown cows are drowsing on their feet, heads down, or browsing near the fence on slopes where the woods' shadow falls. I watch a flycatcher on a limb across the river. The air is so fat with food that this flycatcher never leaves its perch; it simply turns its head, snaps its beak, and dines.

Two things are distracting me. One is a gang of carp on the river bottom; I can see the carp where the sycamore boughs cast shade. During times of excess leisure like this, you can see not only fish, but also a loose-knit network of sunlight on fishes' backs. The same moving pattern falls on the stony river bottom. It looks as though someone has cast over the fish a throw net made of sunlight. Some people eat carp.

Near the bank at my feet is a sunny backwater upon which dozens of water striders are water striding about. They seem to be rushing so they don't fall in. I soon discover that these insects are actually skidding along on the underside of a cloud. The water here is reflecting a patch of sky and a complete cumulus cloud. It is on the bottom of this cloud that the water striders are foraging. They are the size of biplanes or prehistoric birds.

They scrabble all unawares on a cloud bottom, clinging to this delicate stuff upside down, like lizards on a ceiling.

While these complexities are narrowing the focus of my attention, the dog looks up. I look up. The wide world swings into view and fades at once while I listen for a sound. The dog and I are both hearing it. We hear a slow series of clicks up on the road. It is the child, riding her bicycle up the hill.

The child is riding her bicycle up the hill. I stand and look around; the thick summer foliage blocks the road from view. I turn back toward the river and hear the playing cards slap in the spokes. They click and slap slowly, for the hill is steep. Now the pushing grows suddenly easier, evidently; the cards click and slap. At once, imperceptibly, she starts down. The pace increases. The cards are slapping and she is rolling; the pace speeds up, she is rolling, and the cards are slapping so fast the sounds blur. And so she whirs down the hill. I can see her through the woods downstream where the road evens out. She is fine, still coasting, and leaning way back.

We do love scaring ourselves silly—but less every year. Have I mentioned that my classmates and I are now thirty-five?

There is an old Pawnee notion that when you are in your thirties and forties you are "on top." The idea is that at this age you can view grandly, in the fullness of your strength, both the uphill struggle of youth and the downhill slide of age. I suggest that this metaphor is inaccurate. If there is such a place as "on top"—if there is a sensation of riding a life span's crest—it does not last ten or twenty years. On the contrary, the crest is so small that I, for one, missed it altogether.

You are young, you are on your way up, when you cannot imagine how you will save yourself from death by boredom until dinner, until bed, until the next day arrives to be outwaited, and then, slow slap, the next. You read in despair all the titles of the books on the bookshelf; you play with your fingers; you revolve in your upholstered chair, slide out of the chair upside down onto your head, hope you will somehow damage your heart by waiting for dinner in that position, and think that life by its mere appalling length is a feat of endurance for which you haven't the strength.

But momentum propels you over the crest. Imperceptibly, you start down. When do the days start to blur and then, breaking your heart, the seasons? The cards click faster in the spokes; you pitch forward. You roll headlong, out of control. The blur of cards makes one long sound like a bomb's whine, the whine of many bombs, and you know your course is fatal.

Now the world swings into view again. I shift my weight. The cumulus cloud has dissolved in the river. The water striders have lost their grip on the heavens. One by one they seemed to have slipped from the sky, somersaulted in the air, and landed on their feet in this backwater under the sycamore. The carp are stirring up silt from the bottom. The cows are apparently moribund; the dog is at standby alert.

Here it comes again. The child has gone around the loop of roads and is climbing the hill once more. I turn toward the cottage, thinking she might be coming down the drive. But there she goes again, down the hill. She really does sound like the London blitz.

This is limestone country. That means the dairy farmers lose a cow every few years; the cows, poor things, fall through their pastures when the underground roofs collapse. They break their legs or worse and die there of shock, I guess, or blood loss, or thirst, or else the farmers shoot them there. I once saw one of these cows which had fallen through.

Many years ago, walking far downstream where the land is clear, I came across one of these cows, a golden Guernsey lying down in a pasture with her back toward me. I only discovered that she was in fact *in absentia* by walking around to her front and seeing that she had no insides. She had not so much as *one* inside that I could see. Her eyes were gone down to the bone, and her udder and belly were opened and empty; there was her backbone. She was dry leather on a frame, like a kettledrum. Her mouth was open and there was nothing in it but teeth. Instead of the roof of her mouth I saw the dark, dry pan of her skull. Both her front legs were broken. They were stuck in the same hole in the ground—a hole two feet across, limestone shards with grass growing on them. The hole was as jagged as a poked egg. How could she have known which step was the false one?

I backed away. Trying to spread my weight, I made a wide circle around her, the way I had come, hoping the ground would hold me and not having the faintest idea what I would do if it did not, or how far I would fall. Back on the riverside path, I turned. Once again, from the back, that hollow golden Guernsey—old skin-

and-bones—looked, as the saying goes, as though she were only sleeping.

It is limestone country, and toward the town is a mineral springs. Before the turn of the century, people from several cities bought farms here, or built summer houses, so they could take vacations near the mineral springs. Some of these summer people retired here and took to farming. The local farmers, a passive lot, accepted the new gentry—so easily distinguishable in town by their plaid shirts and rubber boots. This was, as I say, around the turn of the century.

Soon the valley became, like so many places, the height of fashion among its own inhabitants. The children of the original summer folk moved here, some of them, and raised their own families here. Then the back-to-the-landers of my generation came, and began clearing land for starveling farms. By then, most of the original farmers had moved to the cities.

The old gentry families and the newcomers got together. They talked about community. They raised barns; they built a Quaker meeting house and used it to organize the blocking of a power project. They held square dances; they blocked a proposal to widen the highway.

They are a people of profound beliefs. They treat cancer with tea. They have come here to abandon society to its own foolishness. They believe in wood heat, unpasteurized milk, and whales. To everyone they are unfailingly helpful.

I meant to accomplish a good bit today. Instead I keep thinking: Will the next generations of people remember to drain the pipes in the fall? I will leave them a note.

Late afternoon: we are inside the cottage now, and baking. I am trying to tell the child a few of the principles by which I live: A good gag is worth any amount of time, money, and effort; never draw to fill an inside straight; always keep score in games, never in love; never say "Muskrat Ramble"; always keep them guessing; never listen to the same conversation twice; and (this is the hard part) listen to no one. I must be shouting— listen to no one! At this the child walks out of the kitchen, goes into her room, and shuts the door. She is this obedient. I have never detected a jot of rebellion in her. If she stays this way she is doomed. On the other hand, I wonder: did she do it for the gag? Even so.

We are baking a cake for Count Noah Very, the neighbor. Here a concern for truth forces me to confess that although I am writing in the present tense, actually some years have elapsed since this weekend in the country. In the course of those years, Noah Very has died. He died of a stroke, and, sadly, was not mourned by kin. His death, of course, makes me recall him with more fondness than I felt for him while he lived, for in truth he was a grouch who despised everyone.

It has been almost thirty years since Noah Very walked us children up to Carson's Castle. Now Noah is in his seventies. He is a hermit who hides in the woods. He is a direct descendant of Jones Very, the transcendentalist poet who composed "The Spirit Land" and other abstracting sonnets.

When Noah was in his twenties, with a degree in English literature from Yale, he had one of his parents' servants' cottages moved to its present location in the woods downstream. He intended, he told me once, to spend a year or two there writing a novel. Somewhere in there he took a false step, like the cow. He got involved milling lumber with which to build bookcases. In his thirties he made a desk. He inlaid the desk's surface with multicolored veneers in elaborate patterns; he carved the drawer pulls in the shape of veined oak leaves. God knows it is your human obligation to admire this desk if you ever visit him and get past the door—and in fact, I never did see such a wonderful desk.

Many years ago his wife renounced him for his adulteries; he renounced their children, who are now variously spoused and dispersed. Over the years he renounced meat, obligation, soap, work, pleasure, ambition, and other people. When the child delivered to him an invitation just before dinner, he was asleep. Like almost everyone, he considers himself an intellectual. He does his shopping when the store opens; if he sees another car parked at the store, he drives around in a rage until it goes away.

He refuses all visitors but young women and girls. When other people come into his woods, he hides and watches them. He hides in the hemlocks; he hides in a silver maple; he hides among clumps of witch hazel. He hides and watches the people knock on his door. He told me all this. The interesting part is why people visit him at all. Because he is hiding in the woods, he cannot refuse zucchini squash. He is the valley's sole outlet for zucchini squash.

One woman, incidentally, who brings him gifts of food weekly, and who has not laid eyes on him in four years, told me she likes this feeling of being watched.

Inside the cottage, Noah accepts sherry and cake. He has aged. The bones of his skull are tent poles from which his skin hangs in catenary curves. The back of his skull is small, but his face is large. He is clean-shaven. His bluish mouth usually has a whining or peeved expression, but tonight the mouth, and the man, look pleased. The child, who is feeling particularly charming, has got herself up in a yellow dress; she arranges herself attractively and temporarily on the couch under a side window. Noah sits in a wicker chair by the magazines and explains how he views various magazines. I haven't seen him in years. I notice with some shock that he is wearing a silk shirt.

It is dark. Outside the whippoorwill is loosening up for a marathon. Actually, I know why the child loves Francis Burn. It is because he is the one to whom she has given her love. But why were we given this fierce love? It beats me. I, too, love one. The child writes poems about Francis Burn and leaves them around for me to find.

"How old are you?" Noah asks the child.
"Nine."
"And what grade are you going into?"
"Fourth." She cannot hide a look of contempt. Her whole class is going into fourth grade.
"Do you know I can't keep track of how old I am? I started losing track of my own age many, many years ago, long before you were even born." If there is anything

the child cannot grasp, it is why some adults try to impress her, and why, even if there were a good reason for it, they go about it so badly.

"My children used to think that was the funniest thing, that someone wouldn't know how old he was. Do you think it is funny?"

The child says, "I think it is completely ridiculous."

I am sitting opposite the child, with an ashtray on my lap. Noah, relaxed, is resting his legs on the low wicker table between us.

"One time," Noah is saying, "when my children were little, and we were all living where I live now, I looked out of the window and saw the children playing by the river. There is a little patch of sand on the bank there. The children were all very young, very small, and they were playing with buckets, and pouring water, and piling sand on each other's feet. I remember thinking, 'This is it, now, when the children are little. This will be a time called "when the children were little."' I couldn't hear anything through the window; I just saw them. It was morning. They were all three blond and still curly-headed then, and the sun was behind them."

I looked closely at Noah, who was looking at the child.

"I said to myself, 'Noah, now you remember this sight, the children being so young together and playing by the river this particular morning. You remember it.' And I remember it as if it happened this morning. It must have been summer. There are another twenty years in there I don't remember at all."

He asks how it feels to be here for just a weekend. He explains how well he knows this land and cottage;

his grandfather used to own it all. His grandfather planted the apple tree beside the driveway, the apple tree under which we fixed the bike this morning. Now he is addressing the child overheartily, as if she were three. She encourages this. Later she tells me she thinks he is "stupid." But he catches her off guard. He is lecturing her about his grandfather's apple tree, in which she has not the slightest interest.

He indicates the window behind her—the yard where his grandfather planted the apple tree. The child, to escape his overexcited gaze, turns on the couch, kneels up against its back, and pretends to look through the window at the apple tree—which, however, she cannot see, because it is dark. She is looking instead at her own reflection. I am just across from her, and can see her in the window.

"Do you know how long it takes to grow an apple tree?"

Noah is leaning forward, and all but singing. "Do you know how long it takes to grow an apple tree?

> You'd have to wait
> until you were ALL grown up . . .
> and married . . .
> and had FOUR children. . . ."

She is listening. She hears the hard part, about being all grown up, and married, and having four children. . . . And as he speaks, her eyes slide out of focus, leave the room, and fill with the blank, impossible figures of these strangers. There is a strange, unthinkable female in a yellow dress, and a tall, blank husband beside her. There are these four children of hers. And she thinks, I swear she thinks, I see her eyes widen as she thinks, seeing these blurred children all in a row: The oldest would be older than I am!

I laugh. The child's eyes snap into focus, and abruptly, delighted, meet my gaze in the window. The woman, husband, and four children vanish. The child sees this: inside the near, shadowed outline of her own reflection in the window, a smaller, distant reflection under a lamp—just me, a woman in her thirties, drinking sherry and smoking a cigarette.

The child is holding my eye, which she sees inside the lighted scene inside the breast of her dress. She is laughing because I laughed and she knows why. She looks at me deeply, the way she does, smiling enormously. I put out my cigarette. The child turns herself around on the couch, and together we resume listening to Noah.

Later, when Noah leaves, I am sad not to be seeing him again for what will likely be such a long time. But Noah says, shaking my hand, that I am silly, that at "our age" there is no such thing as a long time. We are saying good-bye on the grass outside the porch; Noah is taking the path through the woods back home. He has refused a flashlight; he has accepted the cake and several books, among them a Fowler's *English Usage*.

Before bed the child and I play several games of spit. She shows no sign of flagging, and it is, after all, Saturday night in this hemisphere, and we are leaving first thing in the morning, so we get out the aspirin again, and find a full deck, and I teach her the pyramid system of betting at blackjack. She likes it. Although it takes many hours of working this system, and much caution, to beat the house by even a little, as I stress, she nevertheless wins six hundred dollars in forty-five minutes, for which the house, by prearrangement, pays sixty cents. Wasn't there something I wanted to write down?

III

Now it is Sunday morning, mid-July, hotter than blazes, the birds half dead and hushed. We are on our way; we are taking a last look at the river. The water seems lower. The water seems lower, and there's a bit of chalk moon over the woods downstream. On the way back we will visit my sister, as we did on the way— my sister, whom I love. We have eaten and packed the car.

It is funny how the occasion imperceptibly changes, like the light, at an inconstant rate. At any given glance you may see that the dog has rolled over in his sleep, or the trees have lost their leaves. Morning drains inexpressibly into lunchtime, or Christmastime. Overhead the geese are migrating, just as they were the last time you looked. You wash the dishes, turn around, and it is summer again, or some other time, or time to go.

The child and I are standing by the river. Circling us is the dog, who has been disconsolate since we packed the car. He keeps coming up with the idea of hiding in the woods, and keeps rejecting the idea. The child and I are standing side by side. Beyond the pasture, the mountains have vanished in haze. The cows are absent. Over the river the sycamore branches hang wooden without wavering; light from the water wobbles around the branches' undersides and flat across the bottoms of their leaves.

"I'm not going," the child says. "I'm staying here." Some speculation ensues about who is in charge of granting wishes. We watch the water striders. We are, alas, imagining ourselves in the future remembering standing here now, the morning light on the green valley and on the clear river, the child playing with the woman's fingers. I had not thought of that before we came, that she would be playing with my fingers, or that we would hear trucks shifting down to climb the hill behind the cottage. We turn to leave.

And leaving—let me add by way of epilogue—we find ourselves on the receiving end of a tiny, final event, a piece of unexpected wind.

A ripple of wind comes down from the woods and across the clearing toward us. We see a wave of shadow and gloss where the short grass bends and the cottage eaves tremble. It hits us in the back. It is a single gust, a sport, a rogue breeze out of the north, as if some reckless, impatient wind has bumped the north door open on its hinges and let out this acre of scent familiar and forgotten, this cool scent of tundra, and of November. Fall! Who authorized this intrusion? Stop or I'll shoot. It is an entirely misplaced air—fall, that I have utterly forgotten, that could be here again, *another* fall, and here it is only July. I thought I was younger, and would have more time. The gust crosses the river and blackens the water where it passes, like a finger closing slats.

2